THE EXCEPTIONAL TEENAGERS' DEVELOPMENT LEAGUE BOOK

THE EXCEPTIONAL TEENAGERS' DEVELOPMENT LEAGUE BOOK

The Most Important Things You Need to Know

Presented in Two Stages

Ellie's Secret Rule
The Muse & the Magic Writing Board

HOLLAND E. BYNAM

iUniverse®

THE EXCEPTIONAL TEENAGERS' DEVELOPMENT LEAGUE BOOK
THE MOST IMPORTANT THINGS YOU NEED TO KNOW

iUniverse books may be ordered through booksellers or by contacting:

iUniverse
1663 Liberty Drive
Bloomington, IN 47403
www.iuniverse.com
1-800-Authors (1-800-288-4677)

Because of the dynamic nature of the Internet, any web addresses or links contained in this book may have changed since publication and may no longer be valid. The views expressed in this work are solely those of the author and do not necessarily reflect the views of the publisher, and the publisher hereby disclaims any responsibility for them.

Any people depicted in stock imagery provided by Thinkstock are models, and such images are being used for illustrative purposes only. Certain stock imagery © Thinkstock.

ISBN: 978-1-4917-8738-0 (sc)
ISBN: 978-1-4917-8739-7 (e)

Library of Congress Control Number: 2016900782

Print information available on the last page.

iUniverse rev. date: 03/30/2016

For Ellison, my granddaughter,

who inspired me to review my collection of essays and books in order to develop a set of principles and super tips that cover the most essential things that youthful high achievers need to know for dealing with people and other concerns, and that they can rely on as guidelines for having wholesome and fruitful lifestyles.

CONTENTS

INTRODUCTION

The Exceptional Teenagers Development League Book is intended to be a valued keepsake for teenagers with a quest for developing themselves to the fullest extent. It should be kept because it introduces unique insights they will do well to have on hand to review from time to time, and to use in later years when they wish to empower another with valuable ideas. The topics presented are not covered in regular courses of study; however, when teenagers adopt the precepts within them as personal guides, they will find themselves empowered with outlooks and enviable life skills that will set them apart from most others.

Although these topics have been addressed in my book *On Being a Better You,* a new element is brought into play about the manner in which people are inspired to do exceptional things. It would have been well if this element had been added to what I have often told others: "That the spark for doing something better stems most often from what someone else has written or said." While this is only partly true, if I had said that this spark may also stem from words and scenes that come to us in dream-like fashion from regions out of this world, I would have been making a more complete statement; as well as pointing out a reality that has not been given the attention or study it deserves.

While I believe most others will agree that dreams may have helpful effects, I, myself, can attest to having benefited greatly from thoughts and ideas brought to me from "out of the blue." Such have occurred during a wide variety of experiences, to include: while in combat, while teaching and training young men and women within and without the educational arena, and especially while working to enter the conversation on education reform with ideas about increasing student achievement and hastening their development.

I have come to believe that helpful ideas come more readily in day dreams when my intention is to improve upon something or to empower others; and that the day and even the night-time dreams that serve to inspire, guide, or warn me concerning something, are brought on the invisible wings of love. In that this help is always positive, I have come to refer to the unseen bearers of the ideas and strategies that have set me apart from others with knowledge and skills on occasion as heavenly-sent muses.

Without lingering on the subject, and telling of muse interventions during two long careers when I really needed help in thinking outside the box in solving unique problems, I must admit that there were also times when I neglected to follow through on the guidance given me in this way. When looking back over these times, my first thought is always, "I wish I knew then, what I know now."

While this thought has been my motivation for giving young people in their teenage years the jump-start I needed long ago, I must give credit to my own inspirational muse for the idea of using the dreaming aspect as a teaching tool; for giving the book a title; and for challenging me to think hard about a mentoring plan that would cause a great number of kids to have an edge over their fellows in the thinking and acting arenas.

Because my thoughts about the mentoring aspect were mixed, this caused me to look back over my many years as a teacher and trainer. In doing so it occurred to me that as with the teaching act, the art of urging others to become exceptional is a three-stage process -- wherein the first two involved foundational mentoring that serves as a springboard for the third stage which involves the individual's desire to learn more and become better. It also occurred to me that proper teaching required a sound introduction to the main area of concern, the involvement of the audience in understanding what is to be learned, and a check to see if the learning objectives have been met.

I felt that these teaching essentials would flow from a basic outline wherein the topic introduced in the first stage would contain a lesson that teenagers of all stripes would see as advantageous to adopt. Thinking such a lesson would clear the way for getting them to adopt the high points of the topics envisioned for the second stage, I felt that the objectives of the program I had in mind would be satisfied, and that the participants would have been given the most important things they need to know to in order to be exceptionally well-grounded.

Realizing that the main challenge would be that of getting Stage One off on the right foot, I saw the first step as that of introducing my targeted audience to the idea that spirit forces intervene in their minds from time to time to spark their thoughts and actions. I believed that if done in an innovative way, the vast majority of the kids involved would come to see the advantage of listening to their better angels when dealing with key life issues. Further, I hoped that these efforts would lead them to become self-starters in mentoring themselves.

As for advancing the idea that some of our thoughts come from another realm, my thinking was that this can be brought to the fore by a non-alarming and informative encounter with a visitor from this realm. Believing that the first message brought would whet the appetites of teenage kids for seeking out information that will give them an edge in having more productive and fruitful lives, all left was to idealize a face for the specter invented to introduce the fundamental truth to be presented.

A face and costume for the muse who would enter the first dream-lesson to the youthful learners I wished to help came into my mind's eye from out of the blue. Surprisingly, I did not have much trouble in making a pencil drawing of this spirit-like character, nor in choosing the first lesson would she bring upon introducing herself to the dreaming teens. I decided that this lesson would be the one that had inspired my granddaughter to be committed to new and more positive ways of thinking and acting -- the "My and Our Rule," and that it would be delivered by the inspirational muse I elected to name "Mentor."

I hasten to point out that while my use of a muse to drive the narrative may seem archaic in style, I feel that readers will indulge my thinking that spiritual or muse-like interventions -- although not generally spoken of in literary works -- are connected in some way with all phenomenal changes for the better. After all, my intention is to be transformative in such an innovative way that it would add to the self-improvement landscape. Fully believing that if this landscape is watered by easily remembered streams of thought and action, the teens and precocious sub-teens who are willing to wade through unchartered reading waters in improving themselves greatly, will appreciate the sage advice presented regardless of the style in which it is rendered.

The phenomenon of a helpful intervention in the lives of people by invisible sources is introduced in "Ellie's Secret Rule," the dream-lesson the muse, Mentor, brings in Stage One. This lesson is intended to explain a process that provides teenagers with a base of knowledge for dealing wisely with the people, places, and things around them. It is also intended to spark a quest in them to enter the special learning regimen Mentor has devised for Stage Two.

The Preface to Stage Two was written for several reasons:

- To connect the two stages, and insure the rule outlined in Stage One is an integral part of Mentor's plan for introducing strategies that can be put to use immediately and used throughout the teenagers lives.
- To point out the method Mentor devised to involve the teenagers to be touched in the art of developing themselves.
- To provide a synopsis of the remaining six topics that will be delivered in dream formats.
- To introduce the special training-aid that would be instrumental in complimenting and reinforcing Mentor's discussions -- the "Magic Writing Board."

As to the effect *The Exceptional Teenagers Development League Book* will produce, I am very optimistic. This is because when the topics were presented to teenage and older audiences, all praised the concepts revealed as mold-breaking. These groups led me to believe that the teens who adopt the ideals developed will set themselves apart from others; and as a consequence, will be armed with skills and insights for dealing with social, educational, interpersonal, and workplace issues that many grownups do not acquire over an entire lifetime.

STAGE ONE

Ellie's Secret Rule

Ellie's Secret Rule

Ellie, almost thirteen, was like a great many others her age that could hardly wait to complete their youthful years. She day-dreamed a lot about her life after these years were over; however, she had not been able to remember any of her day or night-time dreams for very long. Even the few nightmares that sometimes waked her from sleeping were quickly forgotten.

One night, however, Ellie had a dream unlike any of her others. In this strange dream she saw herself watering the flowers and plants her mother had recently placed in the back yard of their home. As this was an evening chore she liked very much, she usually set out to work while still in her school uniform. When she turned to go inside the house after finishing up, an almost invisible figure caught her eye.

As she looked more closely, this apparition changed from being ghost-like to being an easily seen life-sized non-person with facial features that reminded her of a movie star she admired. Ellie felt right away that this fancifully dressed non-person sitting quietly on the bannister of the porch and smiling sweetly at her, was wise and cunning; however, she knew that this was a visitor from out of this world.

Although entranced by this captivating figure that had a cape draped over her shoulders, a book in one hand, and a rolled up scroll in the other, Ellie noticed that the book being held was the same as one she had put in her own library a few years before. This book, *On Being a Better You,* had been written by her grandfather.

Ellie was shocked when this visitor began to speak, and was moved to the point of being almost out of breath by the greeting given her. This was because she was surprisingly addressed with the name given her at birth, although it was hardly ever used by her family and friends.

₪

"Hello, Ellison," said the strange visitor.

"Hello yourself," said Ellie. "Do you know me?"

"Of course I do. I also know of your wish to excel in life. Although you were not aware of it, I've provided ideas to help you deal with a number of problems, and I've also given you words for expressing yourself clearly during your writing assignments on several occasions."

"I've never heard your voice before, so how can that be?" asked Ellie.

"Well, my dear, that is because ideas given you in this way never make a sound as they are not put in your ear, but in your mind. You see and hear me now only because I have come to introduce myself, and to give you a lesson that you will not forget because it will cause you to see a number of things in a different light."

"Are you a fairy, an angel, a wizard, or what?" asked Ellie.

"I am neither of these, my friend; and I'll tell you why:

"Fairies are very tiny imaginary creatures. Although I may be somewhat imaginary, you can see that I am not tiny.

"Angels have wings, as you know. They also guard over people, and sometimes bring messages of good and bad tidings. I have no wings; however, I am the bearer of good news today.

"Wizards are skillful and clever persons who say and do magical things. The things I do and say may seem magical, but they are done in order to help others adopt smarter ways of thinking about and doing things."

"Well, what are you then?" asked Ellie. "Do you have a name?"

"I am normally an invisible sprite that is known as a 'muse.' When going about my usual job of putting ideas in the minds of those I choose to help, I do not show myself when doing so.

"My real name is very hard to pronounce; you may, however, call me 'Mentor.'"

"I am glad to meet you, Mentor. Is there a reason for your speaking aloud and being visible to me at this time?"

"It is because I am on a special mission, and my work is to inspire and guide very young people like you along a path that leads to their becoming even more exceptional.

"While on this mission, I believe it is best to show myself. This is so the kids I visit will have an image of the one who is giving them thoughts for doing things in an ideal way from time to time.

"What do you think about that, my dear?"

"I think it is a great idea. Kids like me will be very happy to know why these kinds of thoughts are given them, and that it is a muse who is helping them out at certain times.

"I notice that you have a copy of my grandfather's book on being a better person. Am I right in thinking that you gave him some help with it?"

"Yes, you are correct. And while I helped to produce some of the thoughts in this book, it is also true that I, along with other muses, have helped him over the years when he was in need of a tip or two for doing something extraordinary in the interest of others."

₪

"Does my grandfather know that you are visiting me?" asked Ellie.

"It is not possible for your grandfather to know that I will visit anyone. He knows only that ways of doing things are placed in his mind to help him deal with certain issues at unexpected times. And although he has no idea how and why these thoughts are brought to him, he sees my work as blessings from a spirit force. "While he does not understand how he comes up with thoughts for some of his writings, his artwork, and his plans, he knows they make his work exceptional.

"As for secrets, I will tell you one: If it were not for the help of a muse like me, there would be no great people in the world. Nor would any of the really great things you know of, or will learn about later, have been done."

"Am I to guess that this is done in dreams?"

"You may say that we do our work dream-like because, like in dreams, we come to people when they are resting their minds and bodies. In that most dreams that come during one's sleep are mysterious enough to cause confusion, some people use dream books in order to try to understand their meaning.

"You should know, however, that because a message that a muse puts into a person's mind is intended to encourage or challenge this person to think more clearly on a certain matter, dream books are of little value in understanding it."

"That's an interesting thing to know, but I don't understand why muses choose to do such things."

"Like me, my eight sister muses are concerned with helping those who mean well; therefore, our work is to inspire such people and give them ideas to extend their knowledge and skills.

"We only deal with persons who have pure hearts, and who wish to do something in a better way. Sometimes, when we wish to do so, we guide them in doing a thing better than it has ever been done before.

"Does that make sense to you?"

"Yes, it does. I believe both my grandfathers have hearts like that. Are you always around to help them do things better?"

"Not always, my dear. As a matter of fact, the visit of a muse is a very rare thing, and the ideas a muse puts in a person's mind always come as a surprise to the person receiving such help.

"When we choose to help a special someone, we always wait until the time is right."

"I see … May I ask how long have you been waiting for me?"

"Not very long; however, I arrived earlier to help little Billy, a boy living down the street from your home who is very much like you were at his age. Since then, I have been waiting for you to come out to do your after-school chore of watering your mother's plants."

"I know little Billy well. May I ask in what way were you helping this wonderful little boy?"

"Yes … As a matter of fact, you may ask anything you have questions about during my visits with you.

"As for Billy, he needed only to be inspired to review several things he had not been able to grasp fully at school, to include expanding his list of first grade 'sight words' so that he could read faster and better."

"Is the lesson you are going to give me about being a better reader?"

"No, it is not. Actually, my task during each of the several visits I intend to make meet will be to pass on tips that will be useful in the schools you will attend, and to give you lessons aimed at inspiring you to obtain and act on special knowledge that will be useful to you now and in the future.

"As for reading better, during one of my visits with you in the near future, I intend to give you a super reading tip. I call a tip 'super' when it allows one to use all of it, or just the part one believes to be personally useful.

"For example, my reading tip called the 'Really Reading Concept,' is a super one because of its usefulness in helping one to comprehend, to write, and even to speak more artfully. I believe you will see the entire tip as one to remember."

₪

"Is there a special reason for your giving a young person like me some inspiring lessons?" asked Ellie.

"Of course there is, my dear. I have been sent to start up a league of young people who have high goals for themselves. As you are one of these youngsters, I have no doubt that you will be selected for membership in this special learner's league."

"How wonderful! May I ask if this league has a name?"

"Yes, it has. This new league of special learners will be called 'The Exceptional Teenagers Development League.'

"The kids listed on this scroll in my hand are those like you who seek to better themselves through learning. When these kids complete my first lesson and accept me as a guide, they can refer to themselves as 'ETD Leaguers.'"

"While I understand that leagues like the League of Nations, the National Football League, and my soccer league were developed to organize and assist those bodies in working together and competing, my guess is that starting up a league of young learners is similar.

"Is there a special reason for this?"

"Yes, there is a very important reason. Because the future of many lands will fall into the hands of those who are children now, these children need to be prepared. That is why I have been given the task of selecting and helping a number of special teenage kids throughout the world who will find themselves developing others.

"If given great ideas to think about and develop when in their teens, the kids I help will be enabled to use their knowledge and skills in making the future brighter when they are older."

"How do you intend to do this?"

"I will do it with powerful lesson tips, my dear! I believe this is a good time to begin the first of these, so let me ask: 'What is the next thing on your agenda for today?'"

"I will start with my homework. Our teacher said that if this assignment is done with care, it will help us be successful on the quiz to be given on Monday."

"My homework tip will come later; however, your use of the words 'my' and 'our' in speaking of your agenda, is pertinent to the tip I intend to promote today. This is because those words have to do with a special rule I feel those on my scroll will see as extremely meaningful."

₪

"Does this special rule have a name?" asked the excited Ellie.

"It is called the 'My and Our Rule.' Although your grandfather developed it for thousands of kids like he once supervised, I am presenting it to those who would be ETD Leaguers because they need to know the full impact of what we muses have elected to call the 'Queen of Rules.'"

"Why do you call it the queen?"

"We call it the queen because it not only marries up with most rules for living well, but principally because it governs all the aspects of how one is to behave when dealing with the objects one claims as his or her own by using the words 'my' and 'our.'

"By objects, I mean those people, places, and things that are referred to when a person uses words like: 'my this' and 'my that,' and 'our this' and 'our that.'"

"As I understand it, this rule guides a person who makes an ownership claim by saying things like: my dog, my backpack, or our home. Am I right?"

"You are exactly right! And while all 'my type' objects require actions that a person ought to treat in a certain way, 'our' type objects always involve others; therefore, they do not require actions that are quite as personal as those in the 'my category.'"

"How does this rule work?"

"I'm glad you asked, because it opens the door for me to pass on a valuable lesson that those who will be ETD Leaguers will need to keep in mind. That lesson pertains to having a sound definition for a word utilized in expressing oneself. Doing so will always help one in saying exactly what he or she means.

"Although there are a number of definitions for the word 'rule,' my ETD League kids should know that rules are made for orderliness -- meaning how things should go -- for safety purposes, and for guiding one's conduct.

"As for your question, the best way to understand the 'My and Our Rule' process is to deal with two questions regarding the objects in one's life:

- "What does one expect of the object he or she puts in the 'my' or 'our' category?
- "The second is what does one imagine the object placed in one's 'my' and 'our' category, expects of the user of these words?"

"Can you give me an example of this process?"

"Of course … We can use your mother in this example. If she refers to the car she owns as 'my car,' these questions are dealt with as follows:

"The first question pertains to what your mother expects of her car. The answer, of course, is that when she turns the key to start her car, she would expect the motor to begin running smoothly right away. She would also expect it to take her where she wants to go without any trouble, and to bring her back home safely.

"In that the second question pertains to what the object expects of your mother, it is easy to think that the car would expect her to:

- "Check its fluid levels and safety features -- the tires, brakes, and lights -- on a regular basis.
- "Keep up its maintenance schedule and take it to the shop for repairs as necessary.
- "See that it is clean and cared for, and looking as close as possible to the way it looked when she first admired it."

"That is a strange way of thinking, but it makes loads of sense to me.

"It seems that the key to dealing with the 'my part' of the rule is simple: While it is good to think about what you expect of the object, it is better to think of what the 'my' object expects of you."

"No one could say it any better, my dear. The most important requirement of the rule is to consider what the object in question expects of you."

"Now, is there an example that helps to explain the 'our' part of this rule?"

"Of course there is … Sometimes; however, this can be a little tricky. This is because the object may fall in both the 'my' and the 'our' categories.

"For example, when your parents refer to their yard as 'our yard' -- in the context of it being family property -- the 'my' part of the rule takes over.

"In such a case, while we know that they expect the yard to reflect on them as good caretakers, it is easy to think that the yard would expect its owners to see that the grass, the plants, and the flowers are watered on a schedule; that the lawn is free from trash and weeds; and that the living things therein are tended to with care.

"But when your mother or dad refers to the yard as 'our yard' -- in the context of it being a part of the neighborhood -- they expect that the yard will show them to be good neighbors who, by keeping their property in good order, are likely to be also good citizens and persons with high values.

"In this case, we can credit the yard for expecting its owners to take steps to keep it looking at least as well as the other yards in neighborhood."

"I believe the point you are making is that when we use the word 'our' in speaking of things like our neighborhood, our town, and our country, we must look to just doing our part in keeping such things looking and working well."

"That is very good thinking, my dear! Supporting such things with their words and deeds is what is expected of users of the 'our' word."

₪

"Am I right in thinking you are going to explain how ETD League kids will be able to use the 'My and Our Rule' in dealing with most of the objects that kids find themselves involved with?

"After all, kids like me do not have cars or lawns of their own."

"Yes, you are right in so thinking. As for explaining the rule, your grandfather took steps to do so in his book. But since kids listed on my scroll are younger than the ones he was addressing, I want them to have a clear understanding of how the rule applies in helping them in their lives. They need a wider outlook for dealing with the many people, places, and the things they care enough about to put them in their 'my' and 'our' categories.

"Let us begin with my asking you to name a few people you would place in your 'my' category?"

"That's easy -- my parents; my granddad, Papa; my teachers; and my friends."

"Good, those will suffice in making my point. Can you now name what you expect of your parents?"

"Yes I believe I can … I expect that they will:
- "Provide me with the things I need, and some of the things I want.
- "Correct me regarding the mistakes I make.
- "Attend as many of the events as possible that are important to me.
- "Give me an allowance.
- "Listen to me.
- "Provide for my future."

"I would say that those are some very proper expectations.
"Now, let me ask: 'What do you think your parents expect of you?'"

"Well, I think that they expect me to:
- "Be tidy.
- "Take good care of the things they provide for me.
- "Do my best in school.
- "Be respectful always.
- "Listen carefully to their advice.
- "Be obedient.
- "Be aware of the sacrifices that they make on my behalf."

"That was well said, young lady. Now, it is easy to guess what you expect of the man you call 'Papa,' but I do not have to guess about what he expects of you. The note he wrote in the book he gave you, makes this clear.

"Do you also agree that his note made it plain that he expects you to:

- "Adopt some life skills he can give you that are not taught in schools?
- "Allow him to play a part in helping to make you a real successful young lady?"

"Yes, I do. When he is trying to show me how to do something better, he always says, 'Let me give you a little tip for dealing with that.'"

₪

Right then Ellie's mind took her back to her sixth birthday party, and to her grandfather's asking her to promise him that before she put this book away in her library, she would have both her mom and dad read the note he wrote to her:

DEAR ELLISON, YOU SHOULD KNOW THAT THE AMERICAN DOLL WAS GIVEN YOU BECAUSE I WAS TOLD YOU WANTED THIS DOLL AS A BIRTHDAY PRESENT. SINCE YOU ARE MY AMERICAN DOLL, I WANT YOU TO ALSO HAVE THIS BOOK. IN YEARS TO COME YOU WILL SEE IT AS A VERY VALUABLE GIFT BECAUSE AS IT CONTAINS MUCH OF WHAT YOU NEED TO KNOW AS YOU GROW OLDER.

BECAUSE I WROTE IT WITH YOU IN MIND, I WANT YOU TO MEET WITH ME FOR A DAY DURING THE WEEK OF YOUR BIRTHDAY OVER THE NEXT FOUR YEARS TO DISCUSS SOME PARTS OF IT. IF YOU ARE FAITHFUL IN DOING SO, I INTEND TO HELP MAKE YOUR 10TH BIRTHDAY A DAY YOU WILL ALWAYS REMEMBER. ALL MY LOVE, PAPA

₪

"Why do you think your grandfather asked you to promise that you would have your parents read the note he wrote?"

"I have no idea why he wanted both of them to read this note. Do you know why he wanted this?"

"Of course I do. Not only did he hope that they would read your book, he wanted to make sure that they remembered to have you spend an entire day with him during the week of your next four birthdays.

"Now, let me ask: 'Was your tenth birthday celebration a good one?'"

"It was the most wonderful time of my life! But you knew that already, didn't you?"

"Well, I knew it was a very happy occasion. Now let's get back to our work. We are not quite finished with our discussion about some of the people we have been speaking about.

"When naming people in your 'my category,' you mentioned your teachers. Tell me then: 'What do you expect of all your teachers?'"

"That's also easy … I expect my teachers will:
* "Help me understand the lessons they teach.
* "Treat me and all the other children with respect.
* "Give me tips for success when I make mistakes.
* "Give me homework, but not too much of it.
* "Be fair at all times."

"I must say you have done well in naming what you expect of your teachers. Now, what do you suppose they expect of you?"

"I suppose they expect that I will:
* "Be present and on time.
* "Give them the same respect I give to my parents.
* "Obey classroom rules.
* "Pay very close attention to the lesson being presented.
* "Participate in class activities.
* "Take all my homework assignments very seriously."

"Excellent! That was well said. Let's do this once more while listing some of the actions that you expect of your friends."

"I expect my friends to treat me like a sister, to keep our secrets, to share in my joys, and to remember my birthdays."

"While there are other things I'm sure you could mention, what do you think your friends expect of you?"

"They only expect me to be a pal, to respect them, and to treat them as I, myself, would like to be treated.
"Is that saying enough?"

"That's enough for me. You have done a good job in naming some of the most important actions that parents expect of their children; that teachers expect of their students; and that friends expect of their pals.
"If you commit to that sort of thinking about meeting the expectations of others you place in your 'my' category, I promise that you will have little to worry about in dealing with people -- to include those you see as unfriendly."

"Meeting the expectations of people around me is something I intend to do from this point on," said Ellie. "Now, I believe you are going to tell me a few things I should remember about how the rule helps in dealing with 'places.' Am I right?"

"Well, that is to be the next subject, my dear; however, there are a few more things they should know about the people you place in your 'my' and 'our' categories.

"As a matter of fact, muses believe that the more you are aware of the varying aspects of an important subject, the more exceptional you become."

"If you going to cover the most important things about the people we deal with, should I take notes?"

"That will not be necessary during this visit. However, in the future, when I identify the groups of people that will always be in your life no matter how rich or powerful you become, you may wish to make some notes about how you intend to deal with those in these groups.

"For now, I want to continue with our discussion; however, my next point may be a little confusing for most teenagers."

"It may be, but I'm sure it is about something I need to know. Please go ahead."

ℵ

"It is essential for you to know that some people -- including those who love you -- will not always do what you expect of them.

"This is because they do not always think as you do, and because they have their own agendas."

"That's not hard to understand, but I cannot see how their being different from me is a problem."

"It can be a very big problem; however, it will not be if you are willing to abide by the most important aspect in dealing with the 'my' part of this rule."

"I'm not sure I understand … Please explain."

"The most important thing to understand about this rule is that it is strictly a personal guide for your own actions.

"This means it is only for guiding how you, yourself, are to treat the people in your 'my' category. It means also that except for when you are a special leader, you have no right to tell any of the other persons within this category how they are to act."

"What do you mean by being a special leader?"

"By this I mean a person who is responsible for all a team or an organization does or fails to do.

"If you are such a special leader, such as a parent, a teacher, or a business owner, you have the right and the obligation to correct the action of subordinates who need your help in increasing their skills."

"Not only do I understand that part, I can see this rule as a good guide for how you should treat others, as well as a guide for how to get along with the people you put in your 'my' category."

"That was well said. Although I feel that you are well on your way to be a valued ETD League member, a little test will let me know for certain if I am right.

"This test pertains to how you see this rule being used in dealing with the places you put in your 'my' category."

₪

"May I ask you to use the 'my' word in listing just two of the places that you consider special"

"That's real easy," said Ellie. "Both my room and my closet are very special to me."

"Now, if you will, please say something about what you expect of these two special places."

"I expect that my room will be seen as neat and well kept, that it will reflect the kind of person I am when my friends and parents enter it, and that it will meet my mother's high standards during her inspections.

"As for my closet, not only do I expect others to admire the special way I organize my shoes and clothing, I expect everything in it to be clean and ready to wear."

"Excellent! Having said that, it is easy for me to imagine that you are aware of what these two places would expect of you, that you intend to keep these things in mind, and that you intend to do your job in treating these and even the other places you will put in this category with care."

"Yes, but places, unlike people, cannot be expected to have agendas. Am I to think that there is no most important thing that an ETD League kid needs to know about 'places?'"

"Of course there is, my dear; however, it is necessary for you to understand the difference between an agenda and what may be called an 'Aversion Factor.'

"An agenda usually pertains to a list of things to be dealt with. When we were speaking of this earlier, we noted that people have their own ideas and plans about how they intend to deal with certain things.

"Now, can you tell me what you believe to be the most important point an ETD League kid should remember about the agenda of others?"

"It is very simply that their agendas will be different from our own sometimes; and, except in one case, we have no right to them tell others how they should act in dealing with anything."

"That is correct. It is something I would think that an ETD League kid ought to always keep in mind. Do you now have an idea about what is meant by an aversion factor?"

"My guess is that an aversion factor has to do with something special that we ought to add to our thinking when dealing with objects in the 'places' category."

"You are on the right track, my dear … Actually, an aversion factor refers to an item that one must be careful to not do in dealing with the people, places, and things of which one claims ownership.

"In other words, ETD League kids need to give all the objects they put in their 'my' and 'our' categories credit for having aversion factors that they should give special thought to in order to avoid problems.

"Let's make a check to see if you understand this point … Although I understand how you normally intend to treat most places in your 'my' category, I will name one of them, and allow you to tell me of how you will deal with the aversion factor you assign to it.

"The place is your locker at school. 'Is there a special thought that comes to you about what you should be careful not to do regarding it?'"

"I think that since its purpose is to keep things safe, I ought not to leave it unlocked after taking things out or putting things in."

"I am happy to say you hit upon the most important point I hoped you would make about the aversion factor of your locker."

₪

"I believe it is safe to go now to the things that a young person is likely to refer to when putting such items in his or her 'my' category, said Mentor.

"Let me ask you to say a word or two about how you intend to treat three items I think you will more than likely put in this category. These three are: your toys and games, your bicycle, and your dog, 'Tangie.'"

"While I don't have any toys, I intend to share my games with my friends when they visit, and allow them to enjoy playing them as long as they like. When play is over, I intend to store them in the place where they are normally kept.

"As for my bike, I intend to keep the tires inflated with the proper amount of air, and to be careful to keep it looking as closely as possible to the way it looked when it was first given to me. I also intend to:

- "Keep it free from rust.
- "Park it properly.
- "Make sure that when it is left unattended, it will be properly chained and locked."

"As for Tangie, I intend to make sure that she is well fed, that she is bathed and brushed with care, and that we spend some time playing together each day."

"You have done well in stating exactly what I would believe your games, your bicycle, and your dog would expect of their owner.

"Now, if you can, please speak briefly about dealing with the aversion factors of these three things."

"Well, as for my games and bicycle, in addition to not failing to take care of them, it is probably not a good idea to leave them unattended or in the way of others. As for Tangie, I must not scold her too harshly, nor play with her too roughly."

"I am very proud of you in understanding the 'my' part of this rule so well thus far."

"By saying thus far, do you mean there is more to say about the 'my' part?"

"Only a little more, my friend … Now, if you can pass my test on how the rule pertains to yourself, we will have said enough about this part.

"In the same way as before, please tell me first what you expect of your teeth and your brain; and then, what you believe they expect of you."

"That's easy! I expect that my teeth will compliment my smile and be free of cavities. I believe they would expect me to brush them in the morning and at bedtime, to use them only for eating, and to make scheduled visits to the dentist. "I expect my brain to help me in thinking, remembering, solving problems, and in assisting me with my speech and with other mental activities. I believe that it expects me to:

- "Get enough sleep.
- "Eat properly.
- "Exercise it frequently.
- "Wear the proper headgear when involved in sports.
- "Never put things into my body that would limit its helpful powers."

"You have passed this part of the test with the high marks I expected you to make.

"If the other kids chosen to be ETD Leaguers are as astute as you are, developing this league will be easier than I imagined."

"I'm quite sure that all of them will be as happy as I am to learn so much."

₪

"Do you think we are ready now to move ahead with the 'our' part of this great rule that has not been covered?" asked Mentor.

"Yes I do; however, in speaking of many of my 'our' type objects, I also use the word 'my' when describing them. For example, sometimes I say 'our team,' and sometimes I say 'my team.'

"How does the rule help me is such cases?"

"Well, the circumstances surrounding situations must be considered because it should be understood that we must share ownership of the people, places, and things we put in the 'our category'; consequently, the guidelines of the rule will differ slightly when we can only claim part-ownership of a particular object.

"What is most important for you to remember is that the entire rule is to guide your conduct only, and not that of others who are involved."

"I understand that part, but I am not clear about how and why the guidelines will be much different just because of the word 'our.' … Can you explain this with an example?"

"I suggest we do this together. Can you start by using the word 'our' in naming some objects in the 'people' category that are dear to you?"

"There are many in this category, but how about: our team, our neighbors, and our friends?"

"I would say those are good ones; therefore, let's look into how the rule can be used as a guide for you in dealing with these three objects.

"If, for example, you referred to a team as 'our team' -- in the context of it being one you play on -- you would also have to refer to the other players as 'my teammates.' In this case, your main concern would be to meet the expectations of your teammates as a fellow player.

"You can see, however, that in referring to this team as 'our team' -- in the context of it being the team representing your school -- you have no direct role to play in making the team successful."

"I can see that, but how does the rule guide me in this case?"

"Well, we have already addressed this question in saying that it is only necessary to do your part in supporting the 'our' category of things with your words and deeds.

"Therefore, the acts of cheering for the team and in actively participating in activities in order to show your support are the only roles open for you to play."

"Now that all this is clear, I can hardly wait to begin dealing better with the 'my' and 'our' objects in my life."

"That's the spirit I am looking for, my dear. Are you ready to move to the final part of this lesson?"

"Of course I am ready, but I am sure that you can imagine my surprise in knowing that there is more to say about this wonderful rule."

₪

"You may remember my saying that there will always be more to learn about any subject. That includes this topic; therefore, there will be room left for you to give the idea more thought even after this lesson is over.

"So far, we have touched upon the objects that we can see and feel; however, there are also objects in both categories that are not visible, nor touchable. We should discuss these because objects even in other dimensions are included in this lesson."

"What do you mean by invisible and untouchable things?"

"I mean things that one claims ownership of in a mental sense, but that cannot be seen or touched. My future, my country, my goals, my God, and even my hopes and dreams, are examples of such things.

"Although the 'our' word may also be used when speaking of these, what is most important is the promise one makes about how he or she intends to play a role regarding such things.

"As you will soon see, the 'My and Our Rule' will help a person in dealing with things that fall in this category as well."

"I have heard people use the 'our' word in speaking of the invisible and untouchable things you mentioned, but the idea of having a rule to guide one with such things is very interesting."

"Actually, the idea of having solid guides for everything in the 'my' and 'our' categories is the main one I am promoting during this visit.
"Can you speak of something you have hopes and dreams about using both the 'my' word and the 'our' word?"

"In using the 'my' word, I would say: 'I hope and dream to be seen as a top player on my soccer team.'
"In using the 'our' word, I would say: 'I hope and dream that our soccer team is able to win the championship trophy.'"

"Very good … Can you now tell me how this helpful rule can lead you in doing your part in causing these hopes and dreams to come true?"

"Well, if I am a player, the first thing the 'my part' of the rule leads me to do is to find out what top soccer players do in playing the game. This would lead me to learn how to do these things more skillfully, as well as to work hard in using this knowledge in order to become an improved player.
"As for my hope that our soccer team wins the championship, if I am not a player the rule leads me to do all I can in cheering for and being an active supporter of the team."

"Congratulations! Your understanding of the great value of this important rule in dealing with the invisible and intangible things you put in the 'my' and 'our' category is much like I expected.
"I would say that you are well on the way to be a star ETD Leaguer."

"Thank you. May I ask if the kids you select to be in the ETD League will see this as a secret rule?"

"No, my dear; this rule is not a secret. It was your grandfather's mind-child, and it is discussed in his book to help others on being better.
"Although he used only one page to describe the rule in his book, and while I feel his description is sufficient to stand on its own, you may be sure that our discussion about it is more complete."

₪

"I must say that I am very happy to be the muse to introduce this rule to you and to those who will also be ETD Leaguers; however, you should know that my mission requires me to pass on a warning that people need to always keep in mind."

"Do you mean by this that there is something dangerous that kids like me should be aware of and avoid?"

"Well, dangerous is not the word; however, I want ETD League kids to be aware of the fact that some mental suggestions given them may be faulty."

"I believe you mean that some things that come into our minds are not always from muses like you, that we need to know the difference, and that we must take care in not acting on what we are urged to do at these times."

"That is exactly my meaning, and it is the essence of my warning tip.

"Because muses choose to come to the aid of those who are wishing to do something better usually in the interest of others, you can always rely on the mental suggestions that come at these times. These urgings come usually when you are at a loss, or at your wit's end."

"Are you saying that other thoughts that are not based on helping others are harmful?"

"Not exactly, my dear … it must be understood that thoughts which compliment what you are thinking are helpful. These come from one's better angels to support questions in your mind; therefore, you may feel free to act on such mental urges.

"You must not, however, act on mental urges of which no thought has been given. Such urges are called 'Impulses.' They come into the mind quickly, and they impel one to say or do something on the spot that is the wrong thing to say or do."

"I think I understand, but I believe kids like me will have trouble telling the difference between a good impulse and a bad one. Is there more to say on this?"

"It may help if I mention a few impulse-related incidents, and after asking you to comment on what you think the outcomes were, I will try to make this point more clear."

"That's fine, please go ahead."

"Since three such incidents come to mind at the moment, I will make only a brief comment about each:

- "First, while driving along a major highway, a man decided on impulse to change lanes. Immediately after putting his turn signal on, he turned onto a passing lane.
- "Second, while giving a speech, an orator decided on impulse to drive home the point he was making by adding a comment that he had not planned to make.
- "Third, after the paint had dried on a landscape painting he had completed, an artist noticed he had missed a brushstroke, and a tiny unpainted spot was left on his canvas without paint. Acting on an impulse, he applied the color he believed would do the job in correcting this oversight."

"Now, what do you think was the outcome in each of these cases?"

"I can only guess that the driver may have had an accident in changing lanes so quickly, and that the orator and the painter also made mistakes in acting on these impulses."

"I must say that you are on the right track, young lady … Actually:

- "The impulsive driver, in only checking his rear view mirror, failed to see the car following closely on his left side; however, an accident was avoided in this instance due to the quick action of the other driver.
- "The impulsive orator, in attempting to reinforce a talking point, made the mistake of adding a thought that came to him while speaking. In doing so, this part of his speech was seen as clumsy, and it also caused him to go past the time given him to speak.
- "The impulsive painter, although able to mix the exact color he needed for the unpainted spot, realized later that it would have been better to leave the painting as it was. Had he done so, his painting had a very good chance of winning the 'Best Oil Painting Award.'"

"The point you are making is clear enough for me, but I'm afraid I will still make mistakes in judging which urgings are impulsive, and which are not."

"I expect that ETD League kids who understand this reality will train themselves to act only on urgings that tend to refine or improve upon what they are thinking about saying or doing.

"Afterwards, when they feel compelled to act on an urge without thinking about the best way to say or do something, they will know it is not from a better angel.

"I believe that this will become clearer when you respond to this question: 'Can you give me some examples of behaviors that you believe teenagers should avoid?'"

"The examples I would list are: back-talking; putting someone in their place, retaliating against another person's words without giving some thought to the best way of opposing this person, and striking out at someone without giving thought to the consequences of such an action."

"Those are great examples of what teenagers and others should avoid doing. Your list has convinced me that the aspect of working to avoid impulsive behavior will be a defining feature of an exceptional teenager."

"It is a tip I will never forget. As a matter of fact, I will make it a part of my own secret rule for being an even better me."

₪

"Can you put this secret rule of yours in words, my dear?" asked Mentor.

"I believe I can … Not only will I use the 'My and Our Rule' as a guide for dealing with the people, places, and things of which I claim ownership -- to include those objects that are invisible and untouchable -- I will always include myself. In addition to this, I will make a habit of thinking of the aversion factors of the objects falling in the 'my' and 'our' categories, and of never acting impulsively."

"That, my dear, is a concept worthy of an ETD League member.

"Now, while most of your secret rule is understandable to me, I have the feeling that you wish to say more about including yourself in this process.

"We have already covered what you think your brain and teeth expect of you, so what else, if anything, do you mean by this?"

"It seems important to me that I should not only work to keep my body parts strong and healthy, I should do the same about what many refer to as the 'Five Senses.'"

"What an interesting thought! While all of what you have said is very exceptional thinking, those comments speak to a strong commitment to develop yourself completely.

"They also speak to your commitment to guard against anything that would impair your systems of tasting, seeing, hearing, feeling, and smelling.

"Now, I must ask: 'Can put your rule into a more simple form?'"

"My secret rule is to remember that the 'my' and 'our' objects in my life include those that are invisible and intangible, and that these have agendas I must respect. I will remember also that there are things I should do and should never do regarding these objects -- to include those involving myself -- and that I should avoid acting on an impulse."

"Excellent! We shall call this version 'Ellie's Secret Rule.' If you are true to it, you can count on winning many friends and on being successful in all you do."

"I hope that it will be okay if my rule is shared with the other kids who will be ETD Leaguers. Is that asking too much?"

"Of course not … I was waiting for you to suggest sharing your rule with others. Since the league falls clearly into your 'our' category of objects, I see your offer to share something dear to you with those in your league as a pure-hearted act of support.

"You may be sure that I will pass it on to all the kids listed on my scroll.

"I must say goodbye for now; however, you should know that all who adopt the 'My and Our Rule' as a guide, can be assured of membership in the ETD League."

₪

Ellie awoke as soon as Mentor disappeared; however, she realized she had only been having a fantastic dream after looking in vain for any evidence that her visitor had really been in her room.

Too excited to stay in bed, she decided to tidy up her room, brush her teeth and hair, dress, and to water the plants in the front of her home.

Upon returning to the house, she was greeted with a smile, a big hug, and warm words from her mother who had been preparing breakfast.

"Good morning, my dear. I've never seen you up and working outside so early on a Saturday. Did you sleep well?"

"Yes, I slept very well … Although I had a very unusual dream that seemed to last all night, I woke up refreshed and in a mood to do something useful."

"How smart! When I went in to wake you, I noticed that your bed had been made, your room was as tidy as ever, and that your closet had been tidied up better than ever.

"Are you expecting friends to come over?"

"No, none of them are coming over this weekend; however, if my homework assignment has been completed by noon, I plan to meet with three or four of the girls at the park for a short bike trip."

"Well, something strange is going on, my dear. Did this dream of yours have something to do with this new you?"

"Yes, it was really a dream within a dream. It is doubtful that I will ever have another as meaningful."

"All I can say is that your being inclined to do household chores and put your homework ahead of having fun with your friends is showing a point of maturity I had not reached at your age … I am very proud of you."

"Thank you, Mom … I hope someday to make you even prouder."

₪

While eating breakfast and making small talk with her mother, Ellie's mind went back to the events of the night. Her excitement in thinking about Mentor's promise to make some return visits caused her to say to herself:

"I'm a pretty lucky girl to have a mother saying she is proud of me. Even Mentor, my own muse, seemed proud that I had adopted a secret rule. It may be that I will develop another when she comes again with another great lesson."

Upon returning to her room and preparing to begin her homework assignment, she realized that she had used the 'my' word in referring to Mentor as her muse. This led her to put her book and papers aside, and begin the exciting mental task of thinking of what Mentor would expect her.

It took only a few minutes for her to arrive at the thought that if she put herself in Mentor's place, it would be a rather easy job to list what was expected of her. This led her to continue talking to herself:

"Mentor would expect me to think about the points given me during this dream, and how they can be used in dealing with the objects in my life. I believe her highest expectation would be that I take some steps to insure that I do not forget this lesson and the commitment I made to myself concerning it."

This caused her to think of the dairy she had relied on it to record the experiences she wanted to remember. After bringing it to her desk, she turned to a clean page, decided on a heading for her work, and began to write:

The My and Our Rule and Exceptional Teenagers

The most important thing about the "My and Our Rule" is that it is a recipe for one's actions in dealing properly with the people, places, and things that one uses the words "my" and "our" in declaring ownership of them.

The my-part of this rule is more important than the our-part because in treating my-type objects one is required to be more directly involved than when treating our-type objects. In treating "our" type objects, it is best to use cheering words and deeds that show one's support.

People in the "my" and "our" categories have their own agendas; and while places and things do not have agendas, it is best to see all objects in both categories as having aversion factors. It follows, therefore, that exceptional teens must be careful to think about what they should and should not do in dealing with objects in both their "my" and "our" categories.

When referring to our own bodies, each part fits into the "my" category. It is important, therefore, to think not only about doing what these parts would expect of you, but also about what you should not do in regard to them. The body parts that exceptional teens should be extra careful about are those that would control their senses of sight, sound, smell, taste, and touch.

Exceptional teens must train themselves to be aware of, and not act on impulses that impel them to say or do something without having given thought to the action because doing so hardly ever contributes to a good outcome.

When thinking of all the objects in our lives of which we claim ownership, it will be well to remember that some of these cannot be seen or touched. Exceptional teens will do well to establish private goals for dealing with such objects.

₪

The last thing Ellie wrote in her dairy must be seen as a statement by a teenager who had grown immensely overnight. It included her secret rule and the best advice she could give to kids like herself:

My secret rule is to remember that the "my" and "our" objects in my life include those that are invisible and intangible, and that these have agendas I must respect. I will remember also that there are things I should do and should never do regarding these objects -- to include those involving myself -- and that I should avoid acting on an impulse.

If kids in their teens commit to adopting the "My and Our Rule" as a personal guide for dealing with the various objects of their affection, they cannot help from setting themselves apart from others, and from winning the respect and admiration of those around them.

STAGE TWO

MAGICAL PRESENTATIONS

PROGRAMMED FOR
EXCEPTIONAL TEENAGER
DEVELOPMENT

The Muse & the Magic Writing Board

Preface to Stage Two

Mentor, the inspirational muse who introduced herself magically to Ellie, the first teenager to be told of her mission, looks back over the great many dream-visits she had made using the super powers that all muses have. Although she considered her visit with Ellie to be the most memorable, it came as no surprise that the visits to the thousands of other kids listed on her scroll were also received with Ellie's enthusiasm. Each of them was delighted to be singled out as special, and to be a part of a major effort that would cause them to become exceptional teenagers.

Having finished the first part of her mission to establish an Exceptional Teenagers Development League with a great number of special young learners throughout the world, gave Mentor a deep sense of pride. Because each of these teens had agreed to adopt the "My and Our Rule" for dealing with the objects they valued, and had accepted her as a guiding spirit, she looked forward to beginning the second part of her training program.

Although convinced that the visits just completed would have the immediate effect of changing the outlooks of the dreamers she touched for the better, her thoughts now turned to the remaining work to be done in building up and empowering her new "my" objects.

Fully expecting that her newly acquired charges would want to know more about the work of muses, she decided that it would be good to explain this before dealing with what must be the major expectation of kids who saw themselves as being members of a special society of learners. That, she knew already would be to be given information in her follow-on visits that would truly cause them to become exceptional teenagers.

Having convinced herself that several lesson-dream sessions would be required, her chief concern was that since most dreams are soon lost to one's memory, those that she would bring may not have a long-lasting effect. This led her to thinking of devising a scheme that would be a guard against the dream lessons she intended to imbed in the knowledge bases of her charges being only brief memories.

After arriving at the solution, Mentor found herself putting it into words:

"In order to help my dreamers adopt the tips to be given them as permanent mental guides, they, themselves, must be involved in the process of remembering the essential elements of the lessons I will bring. It may be that a system of rewards to mark their progress will pay dividends."

Satisfied with the soundness of this approach for the work ahead, Mentor set herself to making mental notes for dealing with the tasks now pressing on her mind:

Number One -- she would dispose of the task regarding the work of muses by first explaining what she meant by saying earlier that there would be no great people, nor any great achievements, without the help of muses. She would do this by simply declaring that muses from the spirit world were the bringers of special knowledge and skills designed to assist those they saw as deserving special help.

After identifying herself as the muse whose work was that of inspiring those who wished with all their hearts to do wonderful things, she would tell them that those so inspired could expect her help. She would also tell them that after completing the lessons she would bring, each ETD Leaguer could depend on future visits from one of the nine muse sisters.

She could feel free in making this prediction. This is because of the promise made to her upon receiving this assignment -- that at least one of her sister muses would use the gift that was her specialty in assisting the kids she had guided when they were involved in attempts to invent something of value, or advance some well-meaning notion while working in various fields of endeavor.

She would explain that while her main specialty was that of inspiration -- meaning to stimulate the mind or emotion to a high level of feeling or activity, her secondary function was to energize and guide pure-hearted persons. She would also explain that such help in the major fields -- speech, music, science, geography, mathematics, philosophy, art, and drama -- was divided among her eight sisters.

Number Two -- Although the rewards system she had in mind as a guard against their forgetting the guidelines and tips given them, she would use Ellie's reaction to her visit as a means to get all the ETD League members involved in their own development.

She remembered that Ellie not only adopted the "My and our Rule" at once, she also took steps to incorporate the high points from this lesson in what she called a secret rule to abide by; and that she had made an impressive diary entry that included a statement that could hardly have been said better:

"If kids in their teens commit to adopting the 'My and Our Rule' as a personal guide for dealing with the various objects of their affection, they cannot help from setting themselves apart from others, and from winning the respect and admiration of those around them."

Although convinced that using diary entries as a means of recording the essence of her dream lessons would work, she was aware of the fact that many teens did not use a diary. She decided, therefore, that this method would have to be injected using the art of magical realism -- acts that combined fanciful, dream-like elements with reality. In employing this art, her task would be to hold the dream in their minds -- to include the notes they made while dreaming -- until the teens had been able to place a refined note in a real diary, or within a notebook or folder used to contain noes they considered worthy of safekeeping.

₪

Now, pleased with a fanciful plan that would serve to help the ETD League members recall the key guidelines in her lessons, she was anxious to begin her training program. Having already decided that all the topics would come from Ellie's grandfather's book *On Being a Better You,* Mentor began to utter to herself the outline she had in mind:

- "The first topic to be covered should be the one I promised them, the 'Really Reading Concept.' Because the vast majority of the world's knowledge is locked away in books or in computer memory, it will be important to introduce my youngsters to this concept. When armed with the tips within it, my kids can use them for comprehending written works, and for becoming more artful writers, speakers, and test-takers.

- "The second topic should be the 'Three Groups of People in Our Lives.' This discussion will be important to my kids because it will not only make them aware of the individuals who will always be in their lives, it will also give them the decided edge they need for having sounder relationships with the people within these three groups.

- "The third topic should be the 'Three Levels of an Organization.' The ETD Leaguers can use the tips uncovered in this session in order to understand how organizations work and how people at these levels are supposed to function. Because they will be in organizations throughout their lives, this lesson will assist them in understanding how they are to perform when they find themselves located within one of these levels.

- "The fourth topic should be 'Reputation-building Essentials.' This will be an important lesson because it points out several key life skills that should not be overlooked. In addition, the tips revealed will serve as wholesome guidelines for winning friends and influencing others.

- "Next, they will need to know about the differences in the personalities of people they live with and work alongside. The discussions concerning the 'Four Major Personality Colors' will allow my teenagers to identify these color personalities, to understand their differences, and to deal successfully with individuals in one-on-one and in group situations.

- "The sixth of these topics, the 'Kindergarten Experience,' will probably be seen as the most important of the dream-lessons. The tips presented in discussing this experience will not only top-off the guiding lessons that ETD League kids need for becoming more exceptional; they will also play hugely in helping them to have a rewarding, wholesome, and successful life."

Now satisfied that the topics outlined would suffice for meeting her mission objectives, Mentor was ready to make her next dream visit. She felt that her readiness was enhanced by the special training-aid used from time to time by the nine sister muses on challenging assignments. As its assistance would surely come in handy in dealing with the vast and diverse ETD League audience, she was delighted by the thought that the "Magic Writing Board" had been especially set aside for her support during the dream-visits she would be required to make.

This board had been the mind-child of her grandfather, a magnificent master magician who reigned as the grand counsel to the "Sisterhood of Muses." It was developed primarily to flash on words, sentences, and short sayings as tips or guidelines; however, because of the unique way in which it produced these effects, it had become the most popular of those in the vast arsenal of training-aids available to the muse sisters.

Its popularity among the muses stemmed from it being totally reliable in flashing on to display the material she and her sister wanted their charges to read during their very brief interventions. Although it is unusual for such occurrences to be other than brief encounters, when assigned to help develop a young prince and princess to assume their royal roles, Mentor had been aided by this board during her work. And while Mentor was astonished by the manner in which the board reinforced these presentations, its power to do even more amazing things had not been fully revealed.

The master magician had programed this board to compliment or reinforce the points and the ideas the supported muse wished to implant deeply in a person's mind; however, in causing it to emit musical and other sounds, to include a speaking voice, and to display added notes and images as if it had a mind of its own, was proof that the magic of the grand counsel to the muse sisters was boundless. In this instance, the master magician intended that the combined work of an inspirational muse and the magic writing board on a mission of great value to the world received his full support. He also intended for this work to be seen as a reform measure addressing important knowledge and skills that everyone should know about for having a well-ordered and successful lifestyle.

Chapter One

When Mentor appeared in the dreams of thousands of her ETD League members throughout the world at the same time, she was attired in costumes familiar to each; and was speaking in the native language of each member. Alongside her was The Magic Writing Board had been programmed to rouse her kids to dream-wakefulness, and to enlarge upon the high points she intended to make.

On the screen of the board the words "Dream Two" were magically displayed in the language of each dreamer.

Her greeting in each dreamer's language went much like this:

"Hello, my friend. I am very happy to see you again, and to welcome you to membership in the 'Exceptional Teenagers Development League.'

"During the dream lesson where I introduced myself, you showed yourself as being worthy to enter my training program by being open to have me as a mentor, and by being committed to use the 'My and our Rule' as a lifetime guide. Adopting this rule completes the first stage of becoming an exceptional teenager; the second stage involves your being given several additional concepts to adopt."

After speaking briefly about her eight sister muses -- to include the roles they play in the fields of literature, science, and the arts -- she thrilled each teenager with words about them being special. She then informed them that those who completed her ETD League Training Program would receive invisible help from time to time by one or more of her sister muses.

She made it clear that the super tips to be given them in their dreams would be sparks of enlightenment to be fanned into flames by their desires to become even better persons. She said that each of her lessons would be followed by a homework-like assignment, and told them to expect to be surprised by the presentations and even the sounds that would be emitted from the board she kept alongside that had been programmed to perform as a special teaching-aid.

₪

As she began her first lesson with a little story, the magic writing board's screen highlighted the words:

The Really Reading Concept

"Once upon a time, the director of a school district's Junior Reserved Officer Training Corps program elected to speak with group sessions of honor students at each of the twenty-five high school programs under his supervision. He always began by asking the members of these groups if they were good readers.

"In that each member was a top student who considered himself or herself an excellent reader, I'm sure you can imagine the responses all gave him. The director, undaunted, informed them that he intended to share his new reading concept with them in order to see if they agreed that it would come in handy throughout their lives.

"This director stated that his 'Really Reading Concept' would take only about six minutes to explain, and that using the concept during their study periods would help with their test-preparation skills. After mentioning the power of the concept in improving their testing preparations, he took advantage of the full attention given him and was able to present the brief lesson artfully.

"At the end of these little sessions, when the director asked the students if they thought the tips given them in this short speech would be useful in their academic pursuits, they always responded with a round of what he saw as grateful applause ... This, of course, told him that his lesson had been a success."

₪

"It should come as no surprise that our topic for this session is the same as the caption now being shown on my board, the 'Really Reading Concept.' While I am certain that it will help you understand more clearly how an author presents his ideas, it is also intended to introduce a mechanism that I am also sure will serve to your advantage.

"I say this because the college students, the educators, and the several professionals who were also given briefings on this reading innovation, were of one accord: all indicated that they would have benefited in several ways from this concept had they known about it at an earlier time.

"Although the purpose of this dream-lesson is to introduce a concept of value, I expect that at its end you will have a concrete idea of how some authors go about presenting their ideas skillfully, and how this knowledge can serve to help you in writing and speaking with increased clarity.

"You should know that the first half of this key reading strategy is imbedded in the four questions now being highlighted on my board":

- *Why do authors write books and articles?*
- *What is the purpose of a sentence?*
- *What is the purpose of a paragraph?*
- *What types of sentences do we find in paragraphs, and what purposes do they serve?*

"As you may not have ready responses to address these questions, you may wish to hear the simple answers I have for each of the four:

- "Authors write books and articles to share their ideas with readers.
- "The purpose of a sentence is to express a complete thought.
- "The purpose of a paragraph is to develop one idea. If a paragraph contains more than one idea, it has been poorly written.
- "The three types of sentences we can expect to find in paragraphs are named: topic, supporting, and concluding sentences. Each of these type sentences has a purpose:
  - "Topic sentences always express the main idea introduced.
  - "Supporting sentences are those within the paragraph whose purpose is to support the topic sentence. Among the ways in which they do this are by providing facts, details, examples, and illustrations.
  - "Concluding sentences are not always used; however, when used they may function in three ways: to restating the main idea, to summarize the information contained in the supporting sentences, and to serve as a transition or connector to the next paragraph."

"You should know also that many authors and speakers use the introducing, supporting, and concluding format in developing their works. For example, authors:
  - "May develop the paragraphs of their chapters using this format.
  - "May develop the chapters of their book using this format."

"It should be clear at this point that understanding the manner in which paragraphs are developed is useful in comprehending what an author intends to impart to readers. What has not been made clear is how the 'Really Reading Concept' can be used as a tool for helping you prepare for an examination.

"As most examinations are based on something that has been written, the value of this concept can be proved by imagining how a wise student would deal with the special homework assignment depicted in the scenario now being shown on the screen of my writing board":

Scenario

A teacher, who has not had the time during class to cover some important points in Chapter 10 in the textbook, informs the students that reading it will be a homework assignment. In an effort to urge them to read the chapter with diligence, this teacher announces that there will be a quiz concerning the high points of this chapter during the next meeting of the class.

₪

"I believe my responses to the three questions now being projected on the writing board will lead to a solid way for you to prepare for examinations":

1. *Having been tipped off on the "Really Reading Concept," what would the wise student do upon opening the textbook to chapter 10?*
2. *If the total number of paragraphs in chapter 10 is twelve, what does this tell the wise student?*
3. *When armed with the answers to the two questions above, what steps will the wise student employ in readying himself or herself for the upcoming quiz?*

"With respect to the first question, although it is not necessary to do so, this wise student would count the paragraphs in the chapter with a view to finding out the number of ideas the author wished to share.

"With respect to question two, by having determined that the number of paragraphs is twelve, this tells the wise student that the author has between ten and twelve ideas to share in the chapter. The reason there may be only ten is because the first paragraph may only serve to introduce be the topic, and the last one may be the concluding paragraph.

"As for question three, the steps that a very wise student would employ are as follows:

- "In Step One, the wise student will locate the main idea in each paragraph and note how the author develops and explains it. This student will keep the dictionary close at hand in order to look up unfamiliar words.
- "In Step Two, the wise student will prepare a set of comprehensive test questions dealing with each idea presented on one sheet, and write out clear answers to these questions on a separate sheet.
- "In Step Three, the wise student will use the two sets of notes for study. If done with diligence, the student will be ready to deal with questions of all kinds during the quiz, to include: true-false, fill-in, multiple-guess, or essay questions."

₪

"I believe you will agree that the 'Really Reading Concept' is a helpful tool in the comprehending arena. This is because it causes the reader to focus on the main idea within a paragraph, as well as on how this idea is supported.

"I believe you will also agree that the responses provided for explaining what a wise student would do in preparing to be tested may be seen as sound guides. It follows that when this method is included in your skill arsenal, it will be useful in preparing for examinations of all kinds.

"I feel that if you wish to have some memory keys for being enabled to discuss this concept, you need only to remember the questions used to start the conversation, its general useful values, and how it can be used by a student."

When she paused, the magic writing board turned itself on to display a chart intended to reinforce Mentor's statement:

The Really Reading Concept

A. *The key to understanding this concept is imbedded in four questions:*
   - *Why do authors write books and articles?*
   - *What is the purpose of a sentence?*
   - *What is the purpose of a paragraph?*
   - *What types of sentences do we find in paragraphs, and what purposes do they serve?*
B. *The paragraph development format is a useful start point for easily understanding most writing and speaking presentations.*
C. *The three steps leading to notes like those idealized for a wise student, can be utilized in preparing for examinations of all kinds.*

"Although the statements on the writing board may well serve as memory cues for discussing this valuable concept, they also bring an end to this portion of my lesson."

₪

As this chart and Mentor faded from view, another note appeared on the screen of the magic writing board:

Special Assignment

Write a brief statement concerning this lesson as a proposed diary entry. This assignment is not to test your writing skills; but to encourage you to make note of tips that will come in handy in the future.

₪

Because time can go by very fast in a dream, it did not seem strange to the dreamers that following a brief fade-out by Mentor, she would reappear quickly. Before she began speaking, her board enlarged itself to display five of the ETD Leaguer's draft diary entry statements that were obviously in line with some special point she intended to cover:

Jonatan's Proposed Entry

The "Really Reading Concept" is helpful because it is a model for reading, writing, and speaking with skill. The fact that a paragraph is used to express an idea fully by using sentences that are constructed with care is an important lesson that will help me in many ways.

Angela's Proposed Entry

The "Really Reading Concept" is a very important and useful one. Not only for understanding how authors make their points and for testing purposes, but also for using what I have learned about paragraph development to make my points stronger when writing and speaking.

Michal's Proposed Entry

The "Really Reading Concept" is one of the most important tips I have received for being successful while in school. I can see how my understanding of it is essential when studying and developing notes.

Jacqueline's Proposed Entry

The "Really Reading Concept" is a super tip because it contains more than one helpful strategy for one's use. I intend to use my knowledge of it whenever I am engaged in serious study, and when I am writing papers that are going to be graded.

Aidah's Proposed Entry

The "Really Reading Concept" is a special guide for being more skillful in writing, speaking, and in preparing for tests. I will use my understanding of it when making notes to link the ideas an author presents within a chapter in order to recall the most important points made with relative ease.

₪

"Although the draft entries just displayed have similar themes, each reminds me of a technique that is useful in the presentation of one's ideas.

"While I intend to say more on the topic of paragraph development later, you should know that each of these entries was written using one of the common ways to develop a paragraph. Although you will learn that there are seven such methods, the one I refer to now is -- by Simple Support.

"The statement now being shown on my board is intended to add to your arsenal of knowledge; therefore, it should be included as an entry in your dairy":

A paragraph may be developed <u>by simple support</u>. This method is used when follow-on sentences give proof or evidence to support what has been stated in the topic sentence.

"Although each of the most common ways to develop paragraphs will be touched on as we progress, before ending this session I intend to take out a little time to touch on a point that may be of interest to you.

"In the writing classes that you may attend you will find that only six common ways of developing paragraphs will usually be explained; however, I have taken the liberty of adding a seventh. In that my time with you is limited, it may be beneficial for you to be introduced to one of these methods in an example.

"Displayed on the writing board is an example of one of these ways that is very effective, but rarely used":

A Paragraph Developed by Definition

While many are fast to say that a child can read on the basis of his being able to pronounce the words in children's' and other books, to say so goes against the dictionary definition of the word: "To examine and grasp the meaning of written or printed characters, words, or sentences." By placing emphasis on the term "grasp the meaning of," this definition is very meaningful. It goes without saying that in most all cases little children have not developed the skill for examining and grasping the meanings of the words they are able to recall and mouth. While this example alone, gives one pause in stating that a certain child can read, it also points to the advantage those who adopt the Really Reading Concept have over those who meet the ordinary criteria for being able to read well.

"Although I intend for you to have all seven of the common ways of developing paragraphs within your arsenal of knowledge, I believe it is clear that this paragraph depicts a way of thinking as well as of supporting an idea.

"If you agree, it will be wise to also include the statement now being shown on my board as an entry in your dairy":

A paragraph can be developed <u>by definition</u> in order to more clearly explain the word that embodies the idea. This way is effective when the definition expands the basic idea, and when the information presented also gives credence to the definition.

₪

At Mentor's wink, the magic writing board flashed off; however, within seconds it flashed on again:

Two Goals Attained

The My and Our Rule
The Really Reading Concept

Mentor was proud that two of her topics had been passed on; however, the idea that the diaries of her kids would also contain two of the ways to develop a paragraph, led her to make remarks that would also make them proud:

"Goodbye for now, but know that I'm very pleased with your work so far. You should know that you and all my ETD Leaguers who have internalized both lessons have reached an important stage in your development. Therefore, all who have adopted these lessons as guidelines will be awarded the ETD League's 'Pawn Degree.'

"While words about this award are depicted on my board, your meeting the expectation that is cited should be taken to heart as a personal goal."

The Pawn Degree is awarded to ETD Leaguers to mark their attainment of the first two goals in their development as exceptional teenagers. This name for this degree is founded on the function of the pawn pieces in the game of Chess -- to always move forward. The expectation is that those awarded this degree will continue moving forward in acquiring knowledge and skills useful in setting themselves apart from others.

₪

As this statement faded from view, so did Mentor; however, the writing board turned itself on again to display three quotes:

<u>*Quotes About Reading*</u>

"Not all readers are leaders, but all leaders are readers."
~ Harry S. Truman

"Once you learn to read, you will be forever free."
~ Frederick Douglass

"Those who have trouble reading are those who have trouble moving ahead
in the appreciation of all that life has to offer." ~ Byron Pulsifer

Chapter Two

As the bells and whistles that interrupted the dreams of some the ETD Leaguers and roused the many others to dream-wakefulness, the magic writing board began to float pictures showing each dreamer at earlier times at play; and more recently with leaders, friends, and with a younger group of kids they knew in a variety of social and educational situations.

Mentor began speaking as these faded, and the words "Dream Three" replaced them on the screen.

"First, allow me to congratulate you on being awarded the Pawn Degree. Next, I should say a word about the quotes left on the writing board at the end of the last dream, and about the scenes just displayed on it. Although I had nothing to do with either, you should know that my board is known to add helpful information on its own from time to time.

"I am sure that the quotes were intended to urge Pawn Degree recipients to examine a quote they read or hear about that strikes them as remarkable, in order to see if it provokes an interesting or useful outlook. As for the scenes showing you with others at various times, you will more than likely come to see them as meaningful during this session.

"Now, before dealing with our next topic, I must remind you that while having the 'Really Reading Concept' to rely on for help with more than one literary activity, it is important to take your understanding of good paragraph development to heart. After all, understanding the mechanics of developing various types of paragraphs is essential to your being able to present ideas skillfully when writing and speaking.

"My hope is that you have come to see that most of your speaking and writing chores will be centered on either expressing an idea of your own, or expounding on a position made by another. Since this is true, and in that we know that the purpose of a paragraph is to develop only one idea, it goes without saying that the better you are at presenting your ideas, the more you will tend to separate yourself from others as being a clear thinker.

"With this in mind, I feel that an opportunity would be missed if I failed to take a little time out before dealing with the lesson I am to bring in order to list the seven common ways in which writers develop their ideas."

₪

At this, the magic writing board lighted up to project a special chart:

7 Common Ways for Developing Paragraphs (Ideas)

1. *By Simple Support*
2. *By Examples or Illustrations*
3. *By Process*
4. *By Analogy*
5. *By Comparison and Contrast*
6. *By Reasons*
7. *By Definition*

₪

After urging her ETD Leaguers to make note in their diaries about the seven ways of developing their ideas as a safekeeping measure, this chart and Mentor faded from view momentarily. Her quick reappearance was a signal that the dream lesson for this session was about to begin. As she began speaking, the topic of the new lesson magically appeared on the writing board:

The Three Groups of People in Our Lives

"During this dream session, I will cover the topic: the 'Three Groups of People in Our Lives.' This topic is important because the edge one needs for dealing soundly with the people within these groups is not generally discussed; however, I see the points within it as essential to those who would be exceptional.

"After this short session you will see that no matter how powerful or how rich you may become, the three groups of people to be discussed will always be in your life. Although this is good to know, it is even more important to have strategies for making your relationship with people within these groups as wholesome and as successful as possible.

"The primary concerns in dealing with this topic are to be able to identify those who are members of each group, and to understand the proper actions that should be taken in dealing with individuals within these groups.

"While some may identify these groups as those above, those equal, and those below us; I prefer to refer to the three as:

- "Those above us.
- "Those alongside us.
- "Those of whom we are responsible."

"With respect to these groups, we must ask ourselves two questions:

- "One -- what types of people do we find in these groups?
- "Two -- what is our role in dealing properly with these individuals?"

"The answers to these questions can be rather simply stated:

"Those above us usually have positions of authority. Among these are parents, grandparents, aunts, uncles, teachers, other elders, bosses, political representatives, and even our peer leaders.

"It is obvious that obedience is required in dealing with some of these authority figures; however, since all are in the category of supporters and benefactors, in playing your role you must show each of them:

- "Respect due their positions and offices.
- "Gratefulness for their contributions and other efforts they make on your behalf."

"Those alongside us are brothers and sisters, friends, other peers, and even our enemies.

"As for your role in dealing with individuals in this group, it is best to apply the 'Golden Rule' -- meaning that you should treat them like 'you would like to be treated.' In addition, since your relationships with some in this group will be close and personal, my suggestion is to use the 'Super Golden Rule' -- meaning that you treat these as 'they would like to be treated.'

"You may be sure that you will be held in high regard by those in the category of being alongside us when:

- "You treat them as special.
- "You are clean, trustworthy, loyal, and cheerful.
- "You are respectful of their traditions and beliefs."

"Those of whom we are responsible include little sisters and brothers, and even friends when you have been selected as the leader among them. While in later times they will include your children, students, employees, and protégés, it is a good idea to add yourself to this category of people.

"It should be understood that your role will be well played in dealing with those whose care, protection, and well-being are your responsibility, if you display:

- "An upright character, understanding, patience, kindness, forgiveness, and a willingness to give them additional chances.
- "A spirit that encourages and assists them in their work."

₪

Before involving her kids in a process that would remind them of the roles they should play when dealing with the people in the three groups mentioned, it occurred to Mentor that Ellie's granddad had written his book for a more mature audience. She felt, therefore, that one part of this lesson may be confusing to teenagers, and decided to address this issue before moving on.

"While I believe my little lecture will help you in dealing with the individuals in the groups of people who will always in your life, you may be a little confused at my saying that it is a good idea to put yourself in the same category as those for whom you are responsible.

"I said this because while you may not be responsible for other individuals at this stage in your life, you do have some personal responsibilities. These include: dealing responsibly with your own care, protection, and well-being; and giving yourself the same considerations, time, and effort that have been cited for dealing with others in this category.

"And while I believe you have a good idea about how this lesson serves as a super tip, the points now being highlighted on my writing board are intended as a simple review of what has been covered":

Review: The Three Groups of People in Our Lives

Group 1 -- *Those above us usually have positions of authority.*
    (In dealing with these, we owe our respect and gratefulness. To some of these we owe obedience.)
Group 2 -- *Those alongside us are brothers and sisters, friends, other peers, and even our enemies.*
    (We use the Golden Rule and the Super Golden Rule in dealing with these.)
Group 3 -- *Those we are responsible for include little sisters and brothers, and even friends that we have been selected to lead.*
    (In dealing with these in individual and group settings and with ourselves, we must show our best sides and present a spirit of helpfulness.)

As soon after these review notes disappeared from the board's screen, another note appeared on it:

Special Assignment

Write a brief statement concerning how you intend to use this lesson.

₪

As in the dream before, the time went by quickly; therefore, it did not seem strange to the dreamers that following a brief fade-out by Mentor, the screen on her writing board would project, in turn, five of the ETD Leaguer's draft diary entries:

Peter's Draft Entry.

Although many of those in the three groups of people that will always be in my life will not expect anything special of me, it is a fact that I use the words "my" and "our" when speaking of most of those I deal with. Therefore, my secret goal is to take steps so as to treat those in each of these groups in accordance with the ideals I have established for dealing with all individuals around me.

Chana's Draft Entry

That there are really three groups of persons that will always be in my life is an idea worth remembering. Because I would like to be seen as thoughtful and caring, I intend to use this knowledge all my life. My secret will be that of taking steps to treat all within these groups as I, myself, would like to be treated; and the special ones within these groups as they would like to be treated.

Abigale's Draft Entry

I will never forget that I am obligated to deal properly with the three groups of people that will always be in my life no matter how rich or powerful I may become. All I have to do is remember what is expected of me in dealing with those above me, alongside me, those that are beneath me in some way, and especially with myself. My secret is to remember that I can always rely on the Golden Rule and the Super Golden Rule for dealing wholesomely with everyone in my life.

Christopher's Draft Entry

It is important for me to remember that the individuals who will be in my life always, deserve being treated in a special way. From this point on, I intend to identify all those who play parts in my life as either supporters, friends, or as those it falls on me to help. Since the onus will always be on me to conduct myself properly, my goal is to be consistent in treating all these within the three groups correctly, and to insure that I never sway from being consistent in treating myself as I would the dearest of those it falls on me to encourage and help.

Pierre's Draft Entry

I will always remember to connect the "Three Groups of People in Our Lives" with the "My and Our Rule." Doing so, makes treating all those around me an easy thing to understand and do. And while going about the business of treating others correctly, my new commitment is to take a special interest in improving and caring for myself.

After allowing time for her kids to read the draft diary entries, Mentor stood speaking alongside the magic writing board:

"I predict that someday you will wish to pass this lesson along to another. In doing so, I am confident that after identifying and giving examples of those who are members of these groups, most of what has been covered will be remembered. "As a tip, I would suggest that if the main point of your lesson is to improve a person's behavior, using examples that pertain to the obligation one has for treating all aspects of his or her own body with special care will come in handy.

"As for my review of the numerous draft diary entries provided by my ETD Leaguers, I consider those that have been shown on my board to have special merit because each alludes to 'steps' being taken.

"While I am certain that the diary entry you settle on will remind you of this dream-lesson and serve as an important guide, my hope is that you will also remember that when you are explaining something in steps or stages, that you are using what is called the 'Process Method.'"

At this, the magic writing board flashed on replacing the five diary entries with this statement:

A paragraph can be developed <u>by process</u>. This method is used when making a procedure clear by explaining it in steps or in stages.

₪

As this note faded from view, the writing board flashed on to display a chart:

<u>*Three Goals Attained*</u>

The My and Our Rule
The Really Reading Concept
The Three Groups of People in Our Lives

As the statement about the attainment of goals faded from view, Mentor appeared to bring the session to an end:

"Goodbye for now, but please know that your work so far has been excellent! You can be very proud in knowing that the goals you have reached will go far in the process of setting yourself apart as an exceptional teenager.

"Before we meet again I advise you to repeat the topics of those three goals often in order to implant them firmly in your mind. You will find that doing so will pay dividends in the future."

₪

When the waving Mentor faded from view, the magic writing board turned on again to display several quotes meant to add to the dream lesson:

<u>Quotes on Dealing with People</u>

"Everything in the world we want to do or get done, we must do with and through people." ~ Earl Nightingale

"Whether it's two people, a department or an organization, teams are the means by which great things get done." ~ Steven J. Stowell

"It is literally true that you can succeed best and quickest by helping others to succeed." ~ Napoleon Hill

"As we look ahead into the next century, leaders will be those who empower others." ~ Bill Gates

"Follow your interests, get the best available education and training, set your sights high, be persistent, be flexible, keep your options open, accept help when offered, and be prepared to help others."
~ Mildred Spiewak Dresselhaus

Chapter Three

A male voice repeating the words "Dream Four," stirred all the ETD League kids to wakefulness. These words were also being flashed on the screen of the magic writing board when Mentor appeared. While she seemed eager to speak, each kid was moved to think that her dress -- seemingly more formal than usual -- was an indication that her topic would be more formal than before.

After congratulating them on making excellent diary entries concerning the last dream-visit, she cautioned them to take heed of the quotes that had been shown on the writing board at the end of that session. This was followed by a comment having to do with the last session:

"I am certain that the refined entry made in your diary will serve to remind you of the fact that there will always be three groups of people in your life. Still, I cannot over-emphasize the importance of your actions in dealing with individuals within these groupings.

"I mean by this that in playing your role within the family, school, social, and work arenas, the burden falls on you, and not any other, to take the steps required to insure that the relationships you build with individuals within these groups are wholesome."

₪

The magic writing board flashed off momentarily; however, as Mentor continued to speak, it flashed on again to highlight the new topic to be discussed:

The Three Levels of an Organization

"You may wonder why this topic, the 'Three Levels of an Organization,' was selected … Well, it is essential for you to have a clear picture of the levels of activity within an organization, as well as an idea of the tasks performed by the people at each of these levels. I am certain that having these views will come in handy as guidelines for you to remember.

"The simplest way to describe the three-level concept is to say that an organization has a top, middle, and bottom, or base; and that the functions of those located within each of these levels rarely change. In that you have been a part of a two-tiered organization called 'The family' from the start, you will come to see that the work within the family construct is very similar to that in more formal organizations.

"In speaking of a three-tiered formal organization like a school district, we can say that the superintendent and board members are within the top level; that the principal, teachers, and counselors are within the middle level; and that the students are within the base level.

"In that the activities conducted at each of these levels are different by design, it is important to understand these differences. This is because when one is aware of where he or she fits in at a specific level within an organization, and commits to meeting the expectations of that level, that person has an excellent chance of succeeding and being elevated within it.

"With this as a background, the identities of workers at these levels of activity or work within all kinds of organizations are as follows:

- ◼ "Workers at the topmost level are senior leaders, managers, advisors, and their staff assistants.
- ◼ "Workers at the middle level are unit leaders, and their staff assistants.
- ◼ "Workers at the base level are primary workers; however, some of these may be assigned team leader functions."

₪

"At the end of this session you should be able to answer three questions:

- • "One -- What are the general roles played by those located within the three organizational levels?
- • "Two -- What are the keys to meeting the responsibilities assigned at each level?
- • "Three -- In what ways can you contribute to both your own success and to the success of the organization?

"The notes now being shown are intended to describe these levels":

The Upper Level

This level consists of authority figures that are entrusted to govern over the major business interests of an organization. This body is usually organized in a formal manner with a leader or chairman at its head.

While the members of this body may be strangers to the workplace procedures of the organizations being controlled, they are selected on the basis of their reputations, personal and business experience, and their special skills. Individuals at this level are utilized collectively in a variety of ways in efforts to achieve organizational success. As examples, they develop strategic goals and objectives, determine institutional policies, raise funds, and establish budgets designed to meet the financial objectives of the organization.

In addition, they provide administrative, logistical, training, and operational support; and maintain an active communications system for receiving reports and passing on information. While doing so, they keep abreast of the administrative and operational status of subordinate organizations, as well as the effectiveness of the subordinate leaders by way of periodic formal inspections.

The Middle Level

Located at this level are the heads of the sub-units. Each leader at this level is credited with being the all-knowing problem-solver, who is not a stranger to the workplace; and who keeps the objectives of the upper level administrators in mind when conducting activities.

Assistants and staff members are responsible for advising the leader, and are concerned mainly with the management and utilization of the unit's resources of time, personnel, finances, property, equipment, and supplies. These also maintain records on the administrative and operational status of all sub-units under the leader's control.

In addition, those at this level establish standard operating procedures for recurring events and activities, and conduct periodic informal check-ups in order to insure that their sub-units meet or exceed the administrative and operational performance standards that will be evaluated by the higher authority.

When there is no superior organization to this body, as may be the case in the family setting, the senior or head middle-level member is responsible for playing dual middle-level and upper-level roles.

The Base Level

This level consists of team leaders and the workers they supervise. Individuals within this body are responsible for knowing their jobs, adhering to organizational policy, obeying all directives, and performing all tasks assigned to the best of their ability.

High achievers at this level are those who operate responsibly in a team-working environment and display mastery in utilizing the tools that are essential in completing their duties. These need also to be meticulous in caring for their equipment items and in trouble-shooting minor equipment disorders."

₪

Mentor, believing that she had put a great deal to be digested on the mental plates of her young achievers, and concerned that they may not have been ready to digest such a high level of information, thought it necessary to put the central elements of this lesson in a nutshell.

Before she began speaking, the magic writing board flashed off; however, it flashed on again to display the thought she wanted them to remember:

Success in an Organization

When individuals are aware of where they fit in at one of the tiers of organizational activity -- the base, middle, or upper levels -- and are committed to meeting the expectations of the role they are assigned, they will be in line for advancement; and their stature, influence, and reputation within the organization will be increased.

"Although it may be some time before you are required to operate above the base level, I believe that the information that has been provided will allow you to complete the special assignment now being shown on my writing board":

Special Assignment

You are to write a brief statement concerning how you see this lesson impacting your life; however, you may include a comment about how it ties in with one or more of your previous lessons.

₪

As with the earlier dreams, it did not seem strange to the pawn degree holders that following a brief fade-out by Mentor, the screen on the magic writing board would project, in turn, the statements of three of the ETD League members:

Marie's Statement

When first joining an organization, the first question I plan to ask myself is: "Where do I fit in?" This lesson not only helps in answering the question about my position level, it helps in answering two other questions: "What are my responsibilities?" and "In what way can I contribute to the success of my organization?" This lesson ties in with the lesson introducing the "My and Our Rule" mainly because these questions refer to things that are expected of me.

Elizabeth's Statement

Knowing that there are three levels of activity in all organizations, and being aware of the level I have fallen into within various organizations, will keep me from guessing about the role I am expected to play. Before receiving this lesson, I mistakenly thought that some of my parents' actions were far too demanding; however, it helped me to understand that they were only taking steps to help me be better. Therefore, more than any other lesson, it seems to tie in with the lesson on the "Three Groups of People in Our Lives."

Peter's Statement

The lesson on the "Three Levels of an Organization" has not only given me a sound understanding of how organizations are established and how they work, it has also caused me to see its connection with the three previous lessons. As examples, it is natural that I will claim ownership of some of the people, places, and things at either of these three levels; that reading, writing, and expressing myself well will come in handy; and if I am to set myself apart, I must use what I have learned about the three groups of people that I expect to find within most organizations.

"Although each of these statements is in line with the thoughts expressed in the numerous other statements that are suitable as dairy entries, these three were singled out because I can see each being connected somewhat with another of the common ways to develop a paragraph -- by Examples or Illustrations.

"As this method will more than likely benefit you in the future, I urge you to include the note now shown on my writing board as an entry in your diary":

A paragraph can be developed <u>by examples or illustrations</u>. This method is used to get a point across when it is difficult to say or explain something clearly, and when one or more examples or illustrations will provide images or pictures that are easy to understand.

₪

Although the smile by the beautiful Mentor was a warming sight, the magic writing board flashed off, and then on again in order to express her being prideful of the progress her kids were making:

Four Goals Attained

The My and Our Rule
The Really Reading Concept
The Three Groups of People in Our Lives
The Three Levels of an Organization

The thought that the diaries of her kids would now contain notes about four of her visits, as well as about another lesson on a technique for presenting an idea, led her to make remarks intended to be helpful as well as cheering:

"In your planning to share this lesson with others, I believe you will have little trouble if you base your discussion on a three-tiered organization you are familiar with, and outline the expectations of people at each level, and explain how one's performance is key to both personal and organizational success.

"I must say goodbye for now, but know that I'm very pleased with your work so far. As you have reached an important stage in your development, you should know that all Pawn Degree winners who also made diary entries pertaining to the 'Three Levels of an Organization;' and about another of the common ways that an idea can be developed, will be awarded the league's next highest degree.

"While I am absolutely delighted in awarding the 'Knights Degree' to my ETD League boys and the 'Dames Degree' to my ETD League girls, I ask that you take pains to add the topic of the goal just attained to the three I urged you to be able to list on the spur of the moment."

At that, the wonderful sounding voice heard upon their awakening was heard again. It announced the degree being awarded and magically called out the full name of each dreaming ETD Leaguer.

₪

The magic writing board flicked off as Mentor was fading from view; however, it flicked back on again to display a note concerning the degree just awarded:

> *The Knights and Dames degrees are awarded to ETD Leaguers to mark the attainment of two additional goals in their development as special learners. The name for this degree is based on the function of the Knights pieces in the game of Chess -- to jump over the other pieces in certain instances. The expectation is that these degree holders will commit to jumping over the obstacles in their way in acquiring new knowledge and skills that serve to set themselves apart as exceptional teenagers.*

Chapter Four

The sound of drums and cymbals that brought the ETD League kids to dream-wakefulness was followed by the sound of the now familiar male voice. This voice was repeating the words "Dream Five" as they flashed rapidly on the screen of the magic writing board.

When the smiling Mentor appeared, she wasted no time after congratulating them on their new degree status, to reveal the thoughts she wished to discuss:

"While it is needless to say that the draft entries I reviewed regarding our last lesson on the 'Three Levels of an Organization' impressed me greatly, two of the ones that were shown on my writing board near the end of your dream lesson reminded me that I should say a little more on this subject.

"While I saw Marie's statement about the first question one should plan to ask when joining a new organization as a fitting one to ask in all settings, I believe that the best drivers for one's success in an organization is connected with the question: 'How do I best play my role in this position?'

"In that I saw Peter's statement as the most comprehensive of the draft statement entries I reviewed, my recommendation is that the thoughts within it be taken to heart by all my Knights and Dames degree winners."

At that, the magic writing board flicked on to highlight Peter's statement:

Peter's Statement

The lesson on the "Three Levels of an Organization" has not only given me a sound understanding of how organizations are established and how they work, it has also caused me to see its connection with the three previous lessons. As examples, it is natural that I will claim ownership of some of the people, places, and things at either of these three levels; that reading, writing, and expressing myself well will come in handy; and if I am to set myself apart, I must use what I have learned about the three groups of people that I expect to find within most organizations.

"While it is not difficult to determine one's level within an organization, I applaud Marie's thinking that the "My and Our Rule' guidelines are useful for meeting her responsibilities within an organization. Although Peter's very interesting statement included even the 'Really Reading' aspect, the point he made about setting himself apart was the main reason for my thinking of something of which you need to be aware.

"One of the most important things to keep in mind is embodied in this question: 'In what ways are you judged within an organization?'

"It is natural that people within an organization cannot escape being evaluated regarding their conduct, their personal performance, and how they get along with others. It follows that organizational leaders -- concerned with the notion that all aspects within an organization will come under scrutiny -- will note the part you play in contributing to the organization's success effort with special interest.

"Although the art of being evaluated well is not a part of this lesson, I should emphasize that it has to do with your fitting in, the quality of your work, and your team-working performance -- the main drivers to evaluations of all kinds. I intend to give a little more attention to this important concept during our very last session together because being evaluation-ready is essential to all who wish to set themselves apart.

"In the meantime, since setting oneself apart from others is concerned with one's reputation; you may find it interesting that my lesson for this time is centered on the building up of one's reputation."

As Mentor continued to speak, the magic writing board displayed the new topic to be discussed on its screen:

Reputation-Building Essentials

"The guiding tips to be presented in this lesson on 'Reputation-building Essentials' are important because they deal with several life skills that are rarely covered in training programs.

"All should know that how individuals are seen by others depends on the estimates they form regarding the manner in which they are liable to conduct themselves when no one else is looking. These estimates are always formed on the basis of: the uniqueness in which people holds themselves, their treatment of others, and how they will most likely deal with life issues in general.

"In that the purpose of this dream-lesson is to reveal key points in having others form estimates of you that are positive, at the end of this session you are expected to be able to cite each of the five keys on which strong reputations are built."

₪

Mentor's board lit up to display these keys as she continued her discourse:

<u>*5 Keys to Reputation-building*</u>

Be Consistent in How You Treat Others
Be Consistent in Your Manners
Play the Games of Life Skillfully
Have Personal Rules
Mind Your Business Well

"The keys I refer to are shown on my board. They should be remembered because they are universally acceptable as sound guidelines for displaying the attributes upon which good reputations are built.

"Although the terms you see were taken from a chart that was developed by an unknown author, the following statements concerning them are intended to be both explanatory and helpful assists:

- "While the word 'consistent,' means being reliable or steady, the act of 'being consistent in how you treat others' is another way of saying that a good reputation is connected with your steadiness in treating others fairly and respectfully.

"I believe it is obvious that the key thought for this act is to treat others like you would like to be treated; and to treat those you consider to be special, as you think they would like to be treated. You may remember these as the 'Golden Rule' and the 'Super Golden Rule.'

- "When we speak of one's manners, we are referring to the socially correct way of conducting oneself. It follows that the act of 'being consistent in your manners', is another way of saying that a good reputation is connected with how you look, express yourself, an act.

"As these manners are the hallmarks of persons of value, it behooves those who wish to be well regarded to display these features in as positive a vein as possible.

- "Because there are many games in life that one must play, playing them skillfully is based on sound thinking. Because the 'Games of Life' that you must play presently include: the family game, the friendship game, the schooling game, the growing up game, the team-building game, and the work game, adopting a general game-playing strategy should be a goal.

"In that each game mentioned may be seen in a different light, it may be well to view these from the perspective of board game players or athletes. In setting themselves apart, the best players keep four essential things in mind: rules, boundaries, prohibitions, and penalties. And while realizing that breaking rules should normally be avoided, they understand that going out of bounds and being penalized can sometimes be used to their advantage.

"They also understand that in order to win on a consistent basis, some basic needs must be met. Although it goes without saying that the need for staying in shape and for practicing and improving oneself are paramount, the other basic needs that are key to the winning of games are: the need for set plays, scoring strategies, strategies to minimize being scored against; and the need to insure that one's team-player role is satisfied.

- "While rules are mainly for orderliness and safety; the act of 'having personal rules' and being constant in displaying them, will go a long way in proving to others that you are bound by sound and respectable standards of behavior.

"Although there are many personal rules, a set that ETD Leaguers are urged to adopt includes: being on time; not engaging in prohibited things; not avoiding your share of the work load; and not allowing others who lie, cheat, or steal, to be a part of your circle of close friends.

- "The act of 'minding your business well' is one of the most important aspects in the act of reputation-building. All who wish others to have a high regard for them are careful to see that their own business is managed as meticulously as possible, and they are careful to adhere to the sage advice of not passing judgments, and not involving themselves in the business of others.

"Since it is clear that you will be engaged with others in the social, educational, economic, and professional arenas, you can be certain of commanding the respect of others as being reliable, trustworthy, and dependable when you are consistent in: staying in your own lanes; in reporting completion of all jobs; in reporting problems using the established information chain, and even in suggesting solutions to the problems being reported."

₪

Mentor, hoping that all she had said about reputation-building would be remembered and adopted as a way of life for her young achievers, now concerned herself with a way to place the five keys firmly in their minds.

She decided that making mention of the learning objectives announced at the beginning of this lesson would help in this respect:

"While I have no doubt that you believe the five keys for building a strong reputation and to guide one's behavior are sound, a review of these will provide an opportunity for me to pass on another tip."

At this, the magic writing board went to work in order display the earlier chart; however, in a slightly different manner:

5 Keys to Reputation-building

(BBPHM)
Be Consistent in How You Treat Others
Be Consistent in Your Manners
Play the Games of Life Skillfully
Have Personal Rules
Mind Your Business Well

"As you can see, the chart displaying the five keys to reputation building has been changed on my writing board. This was done in order to explain a tip about a simple method for remembering things.

"While I suggest that you establish your own recall system, I have found that making up a code word or a set of code letters like BBPHM, as shown on this chart, for recalling points about certain topics.

"Although my preference is to use the capital letters in simple names like BoB to stand for memory aids for the first two keys, I did not do so in this case due to the difficulty of making up simple names using the letters P, H, and M.

"Although I doubt that you would have little difficulty remembering this chart if I had selected the code terms BCO, BCM, PGS, HPR, and MBW AS recall aids, it is also doubtful that you will experience any difficulty in arriving at your own simple code as a memory aid for recalling the keys to reputation-building with relative ease.

"And while I am confident that this tip on developing codes will find a place in your skill arsenal, my sense is that you are ready to tackle the special assignment that is now being displayed on my writing board":

Special Assignment
You are to write a brief statement concerning this lesson as a draft diary entry.

₪

The screen on the magic writing board becoming dull was taken by the dreamers to indicate the passage of time. Therefore, it did not seem strange to them when mentor appeared upon its brightening and began speaking:

"Having reviewed the numerous Knights and Dames draft diary entries, I am happy to say that all of them met my expectations.

"Still, because they remind me of another lesson to be discussed on developing your ideas within a paragraph, the four now shown on my board are in line with this technique":

Anthony's Draft Entry

I plan to repeat the letters BBPHM each morning after I wake up in order to remind myself of the reputation-building keys. Because the 5 keys serve to guide what I believe to be model conduct, they will be useful to me throughout my life as I work alongside and deal with others.

Margaret's Draft Entry

Every morning when I arise I will remind myself of the reputation-building keys by thinking of the letters BBPHM. Although adopting them will serve to help me in dealing with all kinds of issues and all kinds of people; more than anything else, I believe these keys will help me to be a better me.

Samuel's Draft Entry

I will write the letters BBPHM on a paper and pin it to the wall just opposite my bed. This will be my secret way of starting out each day with positive thoughts about doing good, improving myself, and not being a bother to others. At the end of each day when I assess my performance, I plan on being proud of myself after having employed the reputation-building keys to the best of my ability.

Angela's Draft Entry

Winning friends and influencing people will be a rather easy thing for me if I am consistent in using the 5 keys for reputation-building as I live and work with others. Although I may develop a code of my own, I intend to make a habit of thinking of, and of repeating the key terms represented by a code of my choice.

"Having implied earlier that all of the ETD Leaguers' draft entries were excellently done, you should know that the four shown reminded me of one of the seven common ways to present an idea. This way is -- by Reasons."

When the word "reasons" was sounded, the magic writing board changed to display the following:

A paragraph can be developed <u>by reasons</u>. This form is used to emphasize a highpoint by listing the reasons you think as you do; however, it is best to list them logically and in their increasing order of importance.

"While this dream is intended to give you an additional edge on those who are not ETD Leaguers, I am certain that the diary entry you make, along with this note on paragraph development, will come in handy in years to come."

Although the darkening of the magic writing board was a signal that this session was coming to an end, it flashed on again to display the following chart:

<u>*Five Goals Attained*</u>

The My and Our Rule
The Really Reading Concept
The Three Groups of People in Our Lives
The Three Levels of an Organization
Reputation-Building Skills

₪

Mentor's parting words did much to make her kids prideful:

"Goodbye for now, but you should know that your work in attaining these goals has made me very happy."

While waving, Mentor disappeared; however, her writing board faded out only momentarily. It then flashed on again for the time it took for the ETD Leaguers to read the quotes thereon, and then it faded altogether from view.

<u>*Quotes on Reputation-building*</u>

"It takes many good deeds to build a good reputation, and
only one bad one to lose it." ~ Benjamin Franklin

"It takes twenty years to build a reputation and five minutes to ruin
it. If you think about that you'll do things differently."
~ Warren Buffett

"Associate with men of good quality if you esteem your own
reputation; for it is better to be alone than in bad company."
~ George Washington

Chapter Five

A familiar voice cheerfully called out the name of each dreaming ETD Leaguer in order to rouse them to dream-wakefulness, and to signal that the next dream was about to begin. The voice was that of Mentor, who was smiling and standing by the magic writing board with a pointer in her hand. The words "Dream Six" were flashing on and off in rhythm on the board's screen.

After congratulating them on their excellent diary entries, she mentioned that one of the entries caused her think that there was more to say about the last lesson.

"You may remember my saying that the five reputation-building keys were taken from a chart developed by an unknown author. What I did not say was that this chart entitled, 'Lifetime Keys for Success,' had another key listed -- 'Make Yourself Proud.'

"This sixth success key was not selected for our lesson because the term does not relate naturally to the notion of reputation-building; however, Samuel's entry served in an indirect way to show how this term can be used to relate to our last lesson."

When Mentor paused, this entry was projected on the magic writing board:

Samuel's Draft Entry

I will write the letters BBPHM on a paper and pin it to the wall just opposite my bed. This will be my secret way of starting out each day with positive thoughts about doing good, improving myself, and not being a bother to others. At the end of each day when I assess my performance, I plan on being proud of myself after having employed the reputation-building keys to the best of my ability.

"With respect to Samuel's entry, the point to emphasize is that you can be proud of yourself if you are committed to:

- "Being Considerate of Others.
- "Being Considerate of Your Manners.
- "Playing the Games of Life Skillfully.
- "Having Your Own Rules.
- "Minding Your Business Well."

₪

After sensing that the point she wished to impart to her ETD Leaguers had been made, both Mentor and her writing board faded from view momentarily. Her reappearance, no surprise to each dreamer, was a signal that the lesson for this session was about to start.

As she began to speak, the magic writing board came alive to highlight the new topic of discussion:

The Four Major Personality Colors

"The topic to be discussed this time is about the major personality types found in the general population. These are referred to using color designations in order to simplify explanations concerning these four types. As it will not be difficult to find each of these personality types present in even very small groups of people, you should be mindful of this phenomenon.

"The first purpose of this dream lesson is to make you aware of the fact that you will be dealing with people having personalities that are different from yours throughout your life. The second purpose is to pass on tips concerning how to deal with the four major types that you are fated to encounter on a regular basis.

"At its end, you are expected to be able to identify these four easily discerned personality colors. I also expect that you will understand their differences, as well as the need to adopt measures for dealing skillfully with these color personalities in both one-on-one and group situations."

As Mentor continued, the magic writing board went to work by changing its screen to display the colors she intended to speak about:

<u>*The Four Major Personality Colors*</u>
BROWN
GREEN
BLUE
RED

"You should know that the United States Army was among the first of the major organizations to assign color designations for people in our midst that are known to display the major or dominant personality types.

"Still, what is important to keep in mind is that a dominant personality is observable in individuals of all ages and stations in life, and an artful way for dealing successfully with individuals having personalities different from your own is a need."

Mentor continued speaking as the chart on the magic writing board faded from view:

"I found it interesting that in addition to the color designations promoted in the Army instruction, it featured a basic character description for each of the four dominant personality categories, as well as an animal designation that idealizes the feature most notable in each character type."

Upon her saying this, Mentor's words were captured by a chart that depicted the Army's description and animal designation for each personality color:

The Four Personality Descriptions and Animal Designations
Brown: The Builder (Bear)
Green: The Planner (Fox)
Blue: The Relater (Dolphin)
Red: The Adventurer (Jaguar)

₪

"I believe it is best to explain how these are characterized in the Army literature before dealing further with the four major color personalities:

- "Persons having the BROWN personality are called 'Builders,' and are given the Bear designation because they are mainly seen as being strong-willed individuals. For the most part these individuals are straightforward, no-nonsense leader-types. They like to give orders to others, get on with the job at hand, and proceed to the finish line with little fanfare. In addition, they are seen as being more mission-oriented than people-oriented.

- "Persons having the GREEN personality are called 'Planners,' and are given the Fox designation because they are mainly seen as smart and crafty individuals. These types are mainly interested in being informed and in helping others to succeed. They like to ask questions, to solve problems, and to involve others in reviewing ideas. In addition, they are seen as strategic thinkers and as creative and proactive performers.

- "Persons having the BLUE personality are called 'Relaters,' and are given the Dolphin designation because they are mainly seen as unusually friendly individuals. These types usually have deep concerns about how they and others are treated and recognized. Being people-oriented, they like for all to be courteous, to see folk being congratulated for their efforts, and they look to be rewarded for their work. In addition, because their efforts are usually connected with the satisfaction of others, they are seen as good hosts.

- "Persons having the RED personality are called 'Adventurers,' and are given the Jaguar designation because they are mainly seen as individuals who are speedy reactors and fast thinkers. These types are risk takers with a preference for newness and excitement. They like fun things and fast moving activities; however, they are

69

sometimes forgetful and easily bored. At the same time, they are seen as rarely worried about outcomes, and as having very bright ideas."

"While it is certain that understanding the basic inclinations of each color personality category will serve to your advantage, it is necessary to understand that:

- "Each has a primary outlook that seldom changes.
- "Neither category is deemed to be superior to any of the others.
- "Each has a primary disposition or mood -- meaning the state of mind that one usually projects. Being business-like, creative, friendly, and carefree are examples of these mood-types.
- "Each has a prevailing attitude concerning themselves and others -- meaning a state of mind or feeling about how things should be."

"You should also be mindful of the fact that the outlooks, dispositions, and prevailing attitudes of the color personality types are innate qualities; therefore, it is natural that the needs of those with these differing qualities will be quite different.

"In that strategies are needed for dealing with individuals and groups of people in social and work-related situations, it is only necessary to:

- "Take for granted that all four color personalities will be present in groups.
- "Take pains to signal that the sensibilities of differing others are valued."

"In bringing these into play, it may be well to picture yourself planning to conduct a group meeting with the aim of making it a satisfying experience for all involved. In this case it will be necessary to review the characteristics and the outlooks, dispositions, and attitudes that have just been discussed."

₪

When she paused, the magic writing board lit up in order to project four notes, in turn, that put the strategies Mentor intended to pass on in a nutshell.

Instead of allowing the notes to speak for themselves, Mentor, now unseen, read each note carefully:

*"**Brown** personality folk, because they are serious, no-nonsense performers, always relish timeliness and good order during formal meetings. Therefore, if you wish to make a positive impression on those having this personality color, it is incumbent on you to make sure meetings are conducted in a business-like atmosphere. As these folk operate best in well-structured environments, it will be well if you open the meeting formally, and insure that the major tasks identified earlier are dealt with in a straight-forward manner."*

*"**Green** personality folk are happier when things appear organized. Therefore, in order to impress and gainfully employ individuals having this color personality, you should insure that an agenda is on hand and followed. You should also insure that as much information as possible concerning the major issues to be resolved is identified in an earlier announcement. This will please those having this color personality, as well as allow their problem-solving skills to be brought into play before the meeting begins."*

*"**Blue** personality folk are concerned with recognition issues, and with a sense of prevailing niceness. Therefore, you should thank everybody for being present, and give applause to those whose efforts have recently contributed to the organization's success. Those having this color personality will be impressed if your tone is conciliatory and tolerant."*

*"**Red** personality folk like action, speed, fun, and excitement. Therefore, you should make sure that the meetings move along in accordance with the agenda, and that there is room for a period of lightheartedness. In long meetings, to help insure the atmosphere is a relaxed one, you must plan for timely breaks wherein refreshments or entertaining music are on hand."*

As these notes faded from view, the smiling Mentor reappeared. Believing that this lesson would help her ETD Leaguers better understand and deal with their parents, siblings, friends, and others in various situations, she was now concerned about how to bring this portion of the discussion to a close.

₪

"I believe that you would have no problem if asked to identify and speak to the differences in the personality categories discussed, and I feel that you see the need to adopt measures for dealing with individuals in each personality category.

"As there is little more to say on this topic, I also believe you are ready for the special assignment now being shown on my board":

Special Assignment

You are to write a brief statement concerning this mini-lesson, to include how you intend to use it in the future.

₪

Following a brief fade-out and fade-in of Mentor and the magic writing board that indicated the passage of time, none of the dreamers were surprised at seeing four statements on the new screen. Each, however, was delighted in seeing that one of these statements was very much like the one he or she had developed:

Shirley's Statement

The lesson on the four personality types is one I will never forget. I know now that my personality color is Brown; however, most of those in my close circle of friends have colors that are different from mine. Knowing that it is natural for people to be born with a certain personality type will not only help me in understanding and tolerating others, it will also keep me from making mistakes when dealing with these in one-on-one situations, as well as when they are in a group setting. I will try to tone down that Brown part of me that wants to always be in charge, and will develop a personal strategy for dealing in a responsible way with each of the color personalities I detect.

Elizabeth's Statement

This lesson has caused me to see myself as having a color personality that is Red. And while I know that there are both drawbacks and positives connected with such a personality, all I have to do is work to tone down those features in me that cause others to be overly concerned about my success. Knowing that I do not have complete control in changing the dominant aspects featured in my personality, I see the first task ahead is to strengthen my best qualities. In addition, I intend to copy the features that I admire most among other personality types that can be adapted to my thinking and to my manner of doing things.

John's Statement

Using colors and animal designations to identify the four dominant personality types is a great idea because both are easy to relate to and remember. This lesson has caused me to see that my own color personality is Green. It has also helped me in understanding family members and others have different dispositions and attitudes, and that it is natural for them to see things in a different light than I.

Manuel's Statement

Although I have been gifted with a Blue personality color, this dream lesson has allowed me to identify the other three color personalities among my parents and siblings. More than anything else, it has taught me to me more tolerant of others, and to keep in mind the most positive and negative things about the other color personalities when planning for and doing things with various people in the future.

₪

As mentor was mentioning that while the statements shown did not directly embody the "comparison and contrast" method, they reminded her of a note that should be mentioned again.

Her board was quick to flick off and on again to display this note:

A paragraph can be developed by <u>comparison and contrast</u>. This method is used when describing abstract ideas. The three forms available in doing so are: comparisons or similarities, contrasts or dissimilarities, and a combination of comparisons and contrasts.

When this statement begin to fade, it became clear that this session was fast drawing to a close. Still, it was not surprising to her kids that a chart marking the progress they were making would flash on the board to depict the topics of the goals that had been attained:

<u>*Six Goals Attained*</u>

The My and Our Rule
The Really Reading Concept
The Three Groups of People in Our Lives
The Three Levels of an Organization
Reputation-Building Skills
The Four Major Personality Colors

₪

The smiling Mentor held up six fingers to signal her pride in the ETD Leaguers accomplishments. This was followed by her parting words:

"I am certain that the diary entry you develop will remind you of this sixth lesson and its value. As for the note you added about developing a paragraph, you may be sure that it will come in handy as a method for expounding on an idea.

"If the time comes when you see the need to share this lesson with others, I believe you will have little trouble if you begin by reviewing your notes on the topic discussed in this session, and then by using your imagination provide examples of how you think four people having the dominant personalities discussed would deal with simple tasks like making an announcement, dealing with a written assignment, or conducting a meeting.

"With this, I must say goodbye for now; however, as you have reached an important stage in your development, I am happy to announce that as a result of your completing the six lessons given so far, you have earned the ETD League's second highest award -- the 'Castles Degree.'"

₪

After saying that she expected all Castles Degree awardees to be able to name the topics of all six lesson goals at a moment's notice, the waving Mentor faded out; however, a new note appeared on the screen of the magic writing board:

Because the work of Castles in the game of Chess is to be towers of power that can move in either direction, ETD Leaguers who have been awarded the Castles Degree have shown themselves to be teenagers committed to employ the first six lessons derived from their special dreams as lifetime guides. As this award is given to dedicated learners, the expectation is that each recipient will continue to seek out avenues leading to new knowledge and skills that are useful in playing the many games of life.

♫

After a few seconds, both Mentor and her magic writing board disappeared.

Chapter Six

After they had been roused in their sleep by softly playing piano notes, Mentor entered the dreams of her Castle Degree members seemingly more cheerful than ever before announcing the words "Dream Six" over and over in tune with the piano notes. Even her face seemed brighter than ever before.

Upon her congratulating them for their excellent diary entries on the topic on the "Four Major Personality Colors," and upon her saying that all who had earned the second highest ETD League degree would be given special attention by her sister muses, Mentor's new brightness became clear to the dreamers.

As she was about to introduce the seventh lesson that would bring closure to the ETD League training program, the magic writing board flashed on to display the new topic to be discussed:

The Kindergarten Experience

"I bet you are greatly surprised that the final topic to be covered is based on an experience you had several years ago! I saved it for last because I believe it to be among the most meaningful of all the topics in our training program.

"This topic stems from Ellie's grandfather's curiosity about the statement, 'All I really need to know I learned in kindergarten.' Curious to know why someone would take such a profound position, his research led him to find that this statement was actually the title of a book by an American author, Robert Fulgrum.

"During his review of this book and seeing that it contained a collection of essays where sixteen simplistic concepts were listed and explained, Ellie's grandfather realized that this book spoke to things he, himself, had been taught when very young. In noticing that the topics included such things as: 'Play fair,' 'Wash your hands before you eat,' 'Don't hit people,' and 'Put things back where you found them,' he decided to make a study to determine if lessons with deeper meanings could be derived from the complete kindergarten experience.

"As a result of this study, he concluded that while it is not touted as such, the kindergarten program should be seen as ranking first in importance of all formal training programs. This conclusion was reached because he believed that this early learning experience -- involving the building up of home, school, social, and workplace skills -- serves to set the stage for dealing wholesomely with situations that are encountered throughout one's lifetime.

"It is important to note that Ellie's grandfather's findings led him to determine that there are at least seven major life skill principles that can be derived from this early learning period, as well as to the name he chose for writing about these principles -- the 'Kindergarten Experience.'

"Although he listed these principles as tenets that serve as important guides for individuals of all ages and stations, I feel that his clever method of connecting this long-ago experience with present-day and even latter-day concerns should be given the attention it deserves in all our basic training programs.

"At the end of this session I expect that you will see these connections clearly, and that you will see the value of each tenet in enabling you to develop a wholesome lifestyle."

₪

After completing these remarks, a strange thing happened: As the magic writing board brightened itself, it vibrated in rhythm with the wonderful sound made by a melodious voice emanating from the screen. This voice urged each ETD Leaguer to listen closely to the important lesson to be presented.

Without speaking during the long discourse that followed, Mentor stood alongside the magic writing board with a pointer to be used in marking the points being read from the chart by the unseen speaker:

7 Tenets Derived from the Kindergarten Experience

1. *Ask for the help of others when you are unable to do certain things on your own.*
2. *Establish standing operating procedures for doing those things that occur on a daily or periodic basis in order to conserve on time and energy.*
3. *Understand that rules are made for safety, orderliness, and to guide proper conduct; and that you should take pains to not break them.*
4. *Understand that it is not proper to engage in things that are prohibited.*
5. *Understand that you should strive to be an expert in using the tools that are essential to your success.*
6. *Understand that all are appraised and evaluated in some way on their personal qualities and on their job performances.*
7. *Set aside special periods for dealing with daily issues and those that play a part in your safety, health, and well-being.*

₪

As this chart faded from view, the mystical speaker paused; however, when he continued his voice was raised an octave when he announced the topics before carefully reading the information pertaining to each of them on the several charts displayed:

The Need of Others

"With respect to the need of others, it is a fact that during the days of kindergarten a kid was unable to do many things for himself or herself, to include: bathing, dressing, preparing food, or getting to school on his or her own.

"Even now, there are things that you and even much older others -- including our most able leaders -- are unable to do without help. From this, we can gather that the help of others will always be a need.

"It is necessary therefore, to not only ask for help with those things you are unable to understand and do, but also to be extra considerate of those who help out."

Standing Operating Procedures

"With respect to the idea of conforming to a standard, most can remember from back in kindergarten days that routine procedures were established in order to eliminate discussions and instructions about a number of things that were done on a daily basis during the kindergarten years.

"At home, for example, there were times to: do homework, stop playing, eat with the family, go to bed, wake up, share facilities, eat breakfast, and to be standing at the door all ready to be taken to school.

"At school, there were procedures to be followed daily to include: putting away lunches and clothing upon entering the classroom, seating plans, lining-up for movement, and walking on the right-hand side of the hallway.

"This process -- which is best known as Standing Operating Procedures, or SOP's -- is being utilized within dynamic organizations for dealing with work-related issues and in conserving on resources which include time, personnel, equipment, and money.

"It should be clear from this that if you are committed to excellence, you should make a point of establishing a number of energy and time-saving SOP's for handling those things that occur daily in your life, as well as for those that will occur on a periodic basis."

Rules

"In speaking of having rules, most kids will remember that there were several rules to follow at home and at school during the kindergarten years. Among these at school were: raising hands for permission to speak or be excused; putting things back where they belong; not using another's materials without permission; and using titles like Miss, Missus, Mister, and Professor when addressing school officials.

"In that rules are made for safety, to establish order, and to guide proper conduct -- such as being careful to honor others by addressing them by their titles -- they are necessary in all polite societies. The fact is that if there were no rules, we would be living in uncertain and uncontrolled times.

"Although it is obvious that following rules serves to one's advantage, the breaking of rules tends to diminish one's reputation and lead to penalties of one kind or another in many cases. As an example, driving rules are established mainly to promote safety; however, not following them may lead to negative consequences. Among these are: fines, confinement, property damage, injury, and loss of life.

"From this, you can easily gather that, if nothing else, being committed to following codes of correct conduct and adhering to rules, including personal ones, are trouble-saving measures."

Prohibitions

"As for prohibitions, those who went to kindergarten may recall that there were a number of things that kids were forbade from doing. Among these were: no gum chewing during class, no fighting, no tattling, no cheating, and no telling falsehoods. Even making excuses was frowned on back then.

"What is interesting to note is that those things which were frowned on during kindergarten times are still looked on with distaste in your present surroundings, as well as within society in general. With this in mind, you are better off when you adhere to the adage: 'If something is prohibited, it should not be engaged in at any time or for any reason.'"

Using Tools of the Trade

"The rewards for properly using tools of the trade may be traced back to the kindergarten setting. You may remember that your tool kit consisted of a ruler, protractor, colors, pencils, and eraser, and that your proud teachers awarded you a star, some other memento, or a high grade for using these tools skillfully.

"Although the tools we use presently may include computers or other communications equipment, in years to come they may include vehicles, laboratory devices, or reports. At any rate, it is rather certain that rewards of some type are usually in store for those who show skill in using such equipment.

"By this, it should be clear that there is a need to thoroughly understand all aspects of the tools that are essential to your success. It follows that if you have developed skills for trouble-shooting minor equipment breakdowns and for maintaining these with care, you will be highly regarded in the workplace; and opportunities for your advancement will come sooner, rather than later."

The Reporting Process

"For many, the reporting process was introduced during the days of kindergarten. Back then, the reports given were mainly about one's conduct and about how well the lessons assigned were managed. This process included the report card, letters to parents, and parent conferences.

"Even now, it is difficult to imagine that our behaviors and the manner in which we perform are outside the reporting and evaluation arenas. As this will always be the case, being evaluation-ready should be a primary objective in one's life."

₪

At this point, Mentor came on the scene and began speaking:

"You may remember that I mentioned saying a little more on the subject of evaluations during the last dream lesson. The main point I want to emphasize is that it is of utmost importance to learn the nature of the evaluation reports that will be rendered on you.

"As a tip respecting evaluations, the primary areas you will do well to concentrate on are: your interpersonal behaviors -- those involving others; the skill with which you perform your duties; and your individual and team player performances.

"I should say also that the key to great evaluations is to determine what aspects of the three primary areas mentioned will be examined closely, as well as the criteria -- meaning the standard of excellence that you are expected to maintain regarding these three areas."

₪

After Mentor made her point, this melodious voice emanating from the magic writing board took up its discussion after announcing the next topic as it had done before.

Special Periods

"All who remember the kindergarten experience can recall the special periods that were set aside. These included: locker-time, study time, recess, hand-washing time, lunch time, playtime, singing and acting out time, and naptime.

"Because periods such as these can be raised to higher levels of thought and action, it is rather easy to see that there is great value in setting aside special periods for ourselves in the present time and even as we grow older.

"In determining the value of adopting a special period regimen, it is only necessary to consider the benefits these periods provide. As examples, consider how much a student's or a grownup's life will be improved if he or she:

- "Is careful to put things safely away that are not being used?
- "Is consistent in taking out time to study and to relax?
- "Is careful to have a regimen for eating proper foods?
- "Is consistent in taking out time to exercise?
- "Is careful to take time out to play and to practice those skills connected with schooling and with other activities?
- "Is careful about having a proper hygiene regimen?
- "Is careful to get the right amount of sleep?"

₪

The silence that followed and the darkening of the magic writing board's screen was a signal that this part of the lesson had been completed. As Mentor appeared and was about to speak, the board became bright and projected the thought she wanted her kids to keep in mind throughout the remainder of their lives:

Remember This

If it was the thing to do during kindergarten times, it remains so even now. If it was not right on the kindergarten scene, it still is not right.

"As stated earlier, I would have some expectations of you at the end of this session. You may remember that I expected you to see how the kindergarten experience continues to connect with your present day concerns, and that you see the value of each tenet in enabling you to develop a wholesome lifestyle.

"Because I feel that you would have no problem in understanding that this early learning experience will serve to your advantage as the years go by, I believe you are ready for the special assignment now being shown on the writing board":

Special Assignment

You are to write a brief statement concerning the impact this lesson has had on you, and how you see it as a valuable aid in the future.

₪

Once more, after a brief fade-out and fade-on that indicated the passage of time, Mentor and her board appeared again. Alongside the board, Mentor stood speaking:

"I believe you will notice that at least one of the statements being projected on the writing board portray thoughts that are very much like your own. Therefore, you should be as proud as I am that due to this lesson-dream you are stronger and more ready for the future."

Geraldine's Statement

The lesson on the kindergarten experience is probably the most meaningful one I will receive in pursuing my dream of becoming a professional athlete. Because my heart is set on playing a number of team sports skillfully, most of my out of school and summer vacation time has been devoted to practice and play. While I will continue to focus on better preparing myself for success in each sport, the points provided in this lesson will be of great value.

I know now that I will be a better player as a result of: asking others for advice; standardizing daily procedures will save time and energy; concentrating on the aspects of play that count the most while being guided by the rules established; keeping progress records; and setting aside specific times for eating properly, sleeping, and strengthening my mind and body.

Barbara's Statement

I believe that the last part of this lesson on the need to set aside special periods is the most important of the seven tenets derived from the kindergarten experience. I also believe that the act of setting aside these periods is a recipe for having fewer problems during the entirety of one's life, beginning in one's early years. I see it also as the only tenet where elements of the other six may be brought into play during each of the special periods one sets aside.

As proof that the other six tenets are brought into play, the locker time period can be used as an example. With respect to it: others are needed to provide this place for safely storing one's items; there should be set times for opening it; there should be rules and prohibitions concerning it; one should know how to use the materials being stored therein; and the manner in which things in it are used and kept should be evaluated and updated from time to time.

Abdul's Statement

This lesson on the kindergarten experience is helpful to me in many ways. Being the oldest child, and given the duty of assisting my little brother and sister with their lessons and with other things while the three of us are being home-schooled, I will now be more able to help in guiding their development with relative ease.

I will also be able to take the lessons learned from this dream to make our learning experiences more fun and more meaningful. As examples, I will involve my siblings in role-playing that show the benefits of asking for help, of standardizing those things that occur every day, of having rules and avoiding prohibited things, of being evaluation-ready, and of carefully setting aside special periods for a number of things that have to do with a well-ordered lifestyle.

Anthony's Statement

More than anything else, this dream lesson on the kindergarten experience provides a pattern for having a new outlook for dealing with school, work, and other situations. Because of this lesson, I will remember to call on others for help with things I cannot do; establish procedures for those things that I expect to occur on a daily basis; fight to learn the rules and prohibitions involved in all I do; become as expert as possible in using the tools I usually work with; be aware of those things I will be evaluated on; and to set aside certain periods for taking care of those things that pertain to my welfare and happiness.

Holland E. Bynam

John's Statement

Until now, I saw my kindergarten days as just an enriching time in my life for learning to deal with others, and for developing early skills through play and experimenting. When looking back at these times, and connecting the seven principles or tenets that can be derived from this long-ago home and school experience, I see this lesson as a concept for providing guidelines for dealing successfully in social, educational, and work-related situations, and as a formula for living wholesomely.

"As with your own, these statements simply support the idea that this early learning experience is of immense importance. My hope is that it has further whetted your appetite for continuing to learn and develop, and that this lesson will remain with you as the 'Super Tip of Super Tips.'"

₪

Mentor's wink, accompanied by a winning smile, was usually a signal that this lesson was coming to an end very soon; however, her having one finger raised was an indicator that she wished to make another point.

"Although this has been the longest and last of our dream sessions, it would be an error to not make mention of the seventh way of developing a paragraph presenting your ideas -- by Analogy."

The magic writing board went to work to display the note about paragraph development as mentor faded from view:

A paragraph can be developed <u>by analogy</u>. This method is used to explain a concept or thing by describing a clear parallel between two objects or ideas that are quite different, but similar at the same time.

As this note faded, it was replaced by a larger chart. This one depicted the example paragraph developed by analogy taken from Ellie's grandfather's book *On Being a Better You.*
Then, strangely, instead of the familiar booming voice reading off the sentences being highlighted on the new screen, Mentor's voice was heard:

A Paragraph Developed by Analogy

Pain, even the thought of it being brought to bear, is something that all creatures flee from at the earliest possible opportunity. It is closely akin to fear in that it brings about emotions that arise subjectively rather than through conscious effort. A man, who wishes to escape the tyranny of jeers from peers who belittle his ideas, goes into seclusion to bear out

84

his pain in some hidden habitat. When he wishes to avoid the pain of envy from another who may covet his possessions, a man builds a high wall around his residence. In a battle, for fear of receiving injuries or death, some men refuse to fight and cowardly hide themselves or flee the battle scene. Instead of a war declaration, even powerful countries have been known to resort to sneak attacks against another in an effort to minimize or eliminate some danger they fear. Some cultures, in order to avoid the pain of another culture being mixed with theirs, resort to eradication or annihilation of the race that is weaker in war-fighting ability. In the same way -- and perhaps for some of the same reasons -- animals, insects, and fowl, are known to dig holes, construct webs, and build nests in places that offer security for themselves and difficulty for their potential adversaries. The idea of pain-avoidance may also be seen in some of fighting instincts of man and beast whereby some defend their territories against all comers courageously, while some -- like the cowardly hyena -- will only attack in packs or hordes to overcome a defenseless prey that, in fear of pain, injury, or death, can only run away.

₪

After this paragraph was read, the magic writing board became dark; however, it flashed on again in order to display a chart listing the dream-lessons that had been completed:

Seven Goals Attained

*The My and Our Rule **(M)***
*The Really Reading Concept **(R)***
*The Three Groups of People in Our Lives **(T)***
*The Three Levels of an Organization **(T)***
*Reputation-Building Skills **(R)***
*The Four Major Personality Colors **(F)***
*The Kindergarten Experience **(K)***

The constant flickering of the letters at the end each of the goals being shown were obviously intended to make the point that the letters -- M, R, T, T, R, F, K -- could be used to serve as a memory aid. Mentor made this clear by saying:

"I urge you to either write the code letters M, R, T, T, R, F, K in your dairy, or to develop a code of your own that will be useful in recalling all seven of my dream lessons."

₪

As the goal attainment chart faded from view, Mentor, standing by her board with pointer in hand, began with a short speech:

"Although you have done extremely well in showing that you have met the expectations I made at the start of each lesson-dream, my hope is that you will take the following actions:

- "Write down the topics of the seven dream-lessons until they are firmly etched in your memory.
- "Use your diary notes to assist you in reconstructing each of the dream- lessons in your mind.
- "Take steps, as if you are a mentor, to develop at least one of the lessons you have been given until you are able to present it as a super tip to another person."

"I fully expect that whenever you are challenged to identify yourself as one who has completed my training program, you will not hesitate to give proof of this by having the list of the seven topics -- that have been listed as goals -- on the tip of your tongue.

"I must say that I am altogether pleased with important work we have completed together during these sessions; however, my mission cannot be brought to a close without leaving you keepsake. This keepsake is a creed -- a permanent set of principles that will serve to remind you of the goals attained, and of a number of precepts that will be useful throughout your life.

"My challenge to you is to adopt the creed that will be shown next on the writing board right away, and to keep it in a place that will cause you to remember your commitment to it."

THE ETD LEAGUERS' CREED

Having completed the Exceptional Teenagers Development League program, I will continue in my quest to increase my knowledge and skills, and will rely on:

- *The "My and Our Rule" for dealing with the people, places, and things I use the words "my" and "our" in describing my relationships.*
- *The "Really Reading Concept" for comprehending, writing, speaking, and when preparing for examinations.*
- *The "Groups of People in Our Lives" for dealing with those who support me, those who are peers, and those for whom I have some responsibility.*
- *The "Three Levels of an Organization" in determining where I fit in and in meeting my responsibilities when located within these levels.*
- *The "Reputation-building Essentials" for assuring that my personal conduct is seen in a positive manner.*
- *The "Four Major Personality Colors" in dealing with those who have different personality needs.*
- *The "Kindergarten Experience" for having a well-ordered, balanced, and fruitful lifestyle.*

After the dreamers took the time to read the creed, the smiling mentor pointed to the final chart she would present, and before fading out, said:

"I must say goodbye for now, my exceptional friend. This chart is intended to express my pleasure at your good fortune and my hope for your continued success."

Congratulations!

You *are hereby awarded the Royalty Degree for being dutiful in participating in lesson sessions designed to set yourself apart from others. Like the royal chess pieces -- the King and Queen -- you can now stand and move with powers above your peers. The expectation of all awardees of this degree is to commit to the ETD Leaguers' Creed and to continue gaining knowledge and skills so that they will become even more exceptional as the years ahead go by.*

Chapter Seven

The colors that remained flashing when the congratulations chart that marked the end of Mentor's mission faded from view, was a clear indication that the board was acting on its own to hold the attention of each dreamer.

Although Mentor's earlier warning about the tendency of the magic writing board to act on its own in providing helpful additions to her lessons, she, herself, would have been surprised by the bewitching actions it took in going beyond her mission objectives. These began after the flashing colors subsided, and the familiar voice emanating from the magic writing board spoke the words now vibrating on the screen in the higher octave used earlier when announcing a new topic:

Preface to Stage Three

When these four words faded from view, they were replaced by a scene that astonished the dreaming teenagers. In their mind's eye the faces of seven people were arranged in what appeared to be a framed photograph, wherein each dreamer saw an older version of his or her face in the center of the three faces that were above the bottom four faces. Each of these faces was replaced rapidly by another and then another until numerous other faces had been flashed in their places.

The dreamers could only guess that the magically changing faces were those of former ETD League graduates. When the flashing images stopped, and the original seven faces were shown again, a miraculous thing happened. A lighted frame was formed around all but the dreamer's image as each of these began to speak.

These took turns giving their personal versions of the manner in which they would inform others of their status as Royalty Degree recipients. Although each had the tendency to list the topics in the order in which they were presented by Mentor, they usually took the liberty of changing the first of these topics with words like: the "Queen of Rules" and the last of these with words like: the "Super Tip of Super Tips." One of these used a rhyming scheme for voicing his recall of the seven topics.

₪

When this scene faded from view, it became clear that the master magician who programmed this board intended to give it powers above those given to the muses that he counseled. The words and the scene emanating from it were testaments to a power that often amazed even the nine sister muses:

"This dream cannot end without your being given additional advice to assist you in setting yourself apart from others as you continue to grow and develop.

"As you know, the source from whence Mentor's lessons originated was Ellie's grandfather's book *On Being a Better You.* While this book was developed for slightly older audiences, you ought to be made aware of its time-binding value in giving an edge in the knowledge and skill arenas over the majority of their fellows.

"The final chapter in this book is entitled '*Thirty Fail-safe Tips in a Nutshell.*' In this chapter the author made short work of presenting these important tips by addressing each in capsule form."

After pausing, the unseen speaker continued his discourse by reading the title of the chart projected on the board's screen and the words that followed:

Fail-safe Tips On:

Behaving	*Interviewing*	*Modeling*	*Reading*	*Succeeding*
Comprehending	*Leading*	*Obeying*	*Remembering*	*Teaching*
Controlling	*Learning*	*Organizing*	*Reporting*	*Winning*
Coordinating	*Living*	*Parenting*	*Speaking*	*Working*
Deciding	*Loving*	*People*	*Spending*	*Writing*
Dreaming	Managing	Planning	Studying	*You*

"As you are already well grounded in several of these topics due to your recent training sessions, you should be happy that the seven sessions you have completed will come in handy as you develop strategies for being successful in these and other life issues as the years go by."

₪ ₪

The silence that followed as the image of the book *On Being a Better You* replaced the Failsafe Tips chart, was a signal to each proud ETD League graduate that the magic writing board had completed its task of challenging them to set new learning goals.

In that this image remained in their mind's eye for a short time after they awaked from dreaming, they saw the words in the book's title as a challenge to them for continuing on the road to becoming even more exceptional persons by developing themselves to the fullest extent.

On
Being
A Better
You

No Diets
No Exercises
No Treatments
Just Classical Strategies
& Super Tips

HOLLAND E. BYNAM

"All –Around Success In A Nutshell,"
(Promoting Keys For Influencing People And Succeeding In The 21st Century's
Social, Educational, Economic, And Workplace Arenas)

REFERENCES

Armstrong, Michelle. *Manage your Mind, Master your Life: How to Accelerate Your Success in Life and Business.* Santa Anna, California Seven Locks Press, 2006.

Bennis, Warren. *On Becoming a Leader.* Cambridge, MA: Perseus Publishing, 2003.

Black, Howard and Sandra Black. *Building Critical Thinking Skills for Reading, Writing, Math, and Science.* Seaside, CA: Critical Thinking books, 1998.

Bond, P. S. *Junior ROTC Manual.* Whitefish, Montana: Kessinger Publishing Company, 2007.

Bynam, Holland E., *All-around Success In A Nutshell Program.* www. allaroundsuccessbook. com. 2010.

Bynam, Holland E., *On Being a Better You.* iUniverse Publishers, 2013.

Certo, Samuel C. *Modern Management.* Upper Saddle River, New Jersey: Prentice Hall, 2002.

"Dealing With People." Assessed August 17, 2014. http://www.Inspirational Quotes and Poems.net.

Fulgrum, Robert. *All I Really Need to Know I learned in Kindergarten.* New York: Ballantine Books, 1989.

Goss, Jocelyn Pretlow. *Rhetoric & Readings For Writing.* Arlington, VA: Kendall-Hunt Publishing Company, 1975.

Leadership Theory and Application, *Custom Edition for JROTC.* Boston: Pearson Custom Publishing, 2002.

London, Manuel. *Leadership Development: Paths to Self–Insight and Professional Growth.* Mahwah, NJ: Lawrence Erbaum Associates, 2001.

Mount, M., Llies, R., & Johnson, E. (2006) "Relationship of Personality Traits and Counterproductive Work Behaviors: "The mediating effects of job satisfaction." *Personal Psychology*, 59, 591-622.

"Quotes on Dealing With People." Accessed August 17, 2014. http://www. quotesforthemind.com.

"Reputation Building." Accessed August 17, 2014. http://www. Brainy quotes.com.

Webster's New Reference library, Nashville: Thomas Nelson publishers, 1989.

ABOUT THE AUTHOR

Born on his grandparent's farm in Pattison, Texas, Holland E. Bynam has had many firsts in his life. Starting with his being first in his family to complete college, they have continued over the years to include being first of his race to hold a number of key military positions and to win numerous first place awards. Others, along with his noteworthy exploits and successful outcomes, are chronicled in his life story, *An Incredible Journey* (2015).

He is now devoted to continuing the work he started many years ago in the training arena. These efforts involve the sharing of strategies, concepts, and tips designed to help others in setting themselves and their organizations apart from others in knowledge and skills he garnered during his amazing journey that included two long careers.

He retired first from the military in the rank of colonel in 1983 following an assignment as commander of the nation's famous Green Beret unit, the Fifth Special Forces Group. His dynamic military career, included assignments as commandant of three specialized military schools and as professor of military science at the university level. As a result of his successes which included building what was regarded as the largest and the most proficient Reserved Officers Training Corps (ROTC) college program in the nation, he was regarded as one of the Army's top leaders in the training arena.

Upon returning to his hometown, Houston, Texas, to await a school district leadership position, he established a local building construction company with his brother. During this time he was lauded by the Pizza Hut Corporation for his ingenuity in constructing a Pizza Hut site in the fastest time in competition with five other construction companies. Prior to entering his work with schools, he took a position in the city's aviation department and served as manager of its newly established Technical Services Department (1986-87).

His community service work includes: serving on several Texas Gulf Coast boards, assisting and training veterans' groups, and making guest speaker appearances in support of elementary and high schools, three local Texas universities, two hospitals, and at two parent-teacher council conferences. In addition, he has been a Boy Scout commissioner and a long-serving Men's Group president and Sunday School teacher at his church.

He served for twenty years in the Houston Independent School District as a senior instructor, academy director, deputy department director, and as director of its Junior ROTC department. In his first year as department director supervising the twenty-five high school programs in his school district, each of his school programs earned a special honor unit award, and held the distinction annually of being special honor units throughout the seven years of his tenure. Under his leadership this organization was continuously recognized as the nation's top performing large school district program. He retired for the second time as an award-winning administrator after being given his school board's Meritorious Service Certificate for his commitment to students in 2007.

He has been cited for many achievements and has received many awards over the years to include while in the military where he distinguished himself while serving as commander of three unique battalions and in key staff positions at every level including the Joint Chiefs of Staff. Many of these honors stem from his innovative training methods that were chronicled in military magazines, from his personal valorous actions, and from the war-fighting concepts he developed that set his organization apart from others during the war in Vietnam: the "Hasty Defense System," the "Sure Kill" rifle marksmanship technique, the "Modified Eagle Flight" tactic for fast-moving air and ground attacks, and a model battalion fire support base.

While his personal awards include the Silver Star, two awards of the Legion of Merit, five Bronze Stars, and two Purple Heart medals, he proudly wears an unprecedented number of decorations that recognize distinguished unit actions, to include: the Presidential Unit Citation, the Valorous Unit Award, and the Vietnam Cross of Gallantry. Although his civilian awards include: being named Teacher of the Year at both high schools where he served as senior army instructor, he is most proud of being honored by his three Alma Maters. He received a plaque from Norfolk State University recognizing his being first to complete its graduate studies program (2005); was placed on Houston's Phillis Wheatley High School's "Wall of Fame" along with other notables that include his classmate, Congresswoman Barbara Jordan (2014); and was presented with the Prairie View A&M University Alumni Association's Lifetime Achievement Award (2015).

His educational training has been extensive. He received a Bachelor of Science degree in biology from Prairie View A&M University in 1957, and returned to his alma mater under the auspices of the Army to earn a Master of Education degree in the field of the supervision of education in 1971. His Master of Arts degree in the field of interpersonal communications was awarded at Norfolk State University at the end of his tenure as an award-winning professor of military science at that university in 1975. He is a graduate of a number of military schools to include the Army's Command and General Staff College (1970) and the prestigious National War College (1980).

His most notable civilian accomplishments involve his efforts to make inroads in the educational reform movement. These began after his retiring from the secondary school system and after serving in leadership positions during two summer university assignments that involved entering freshmen students. As a result of these experiences, he formed the belief that the student-based problems besetting our institutions stemmed mainly from the students not being successful. He also believed that their not being successful stems from their not being given the motivational tools and help with the life skills needed in order to be successful in the social, educational, economic, and workplace arenas.

Using these beliefs as focus points for a research study, the colonel reached the conclusion that the problems that beset our schools are best solved from within the students themselves -- not by outside resources -- and that what they need most is not covered in regular training programs. This conclusion was arrived at after receiving laudable reviews by educational leaders at every level, and by groups of students at both the secondary and post-secondary levels who were given briefings and introduced to a set of his program books. These were designed to change student outlooks, put a new face on character development training, and increase student achievement.

His records indicate that the educators contacted were of the opinion that the books for the "Super Tips for Success Program" (Student Text, Teacher's Edition, and Workbook) were the most advanced yet for empowering students. After agreeing that this program which would alleviate the major problems that plague our schools and universities, to include: low grades, poor attendance, dropouts, and student-based behavior issues; they urged that it be implemented with all haste. However, due to restrictions placed on educational leaders from adopting or implementing innovative programs that are not developed within the laboratories of universities from which approved programs originate, this program has not been institutionalized.

To counter this oversight, one former Texas Board of Education member advised that the colonel change this program's focus and make it available to students and wider audiences in a success club format. Taking this advice, he developed another set of books for the success club program he envisioned under the heading "All-Around Success In A Nutshell." These books were given the titles: Basic Manual, Facilitator Edition, and Support Manual and Workbook.

Although remaining hopeful that the Success Club Concept will be implemented outside traditional training programs, the colonel believes that since realistic group mentoring programs are not yet in vogue, his efforts should be oriented towards the self-mentoring arena. His website, www.hollandbynam.com, features a plethora of self-mentoring guidelines that he felt would appeal to a variety of audience groups. Among these are a number of blogs addressing the educational reform movement, the success program books, a DVD entitled "6 Supper Tips for Success," and excepts from his book entitled *On Being a Better You* (2013).

The focus of the book On *Being a Better You* is in keeping with the colonel's theme: "That much of what people need to know in order to be successful is not covered in regular training courses." In addressing this theme, he deftly provides easily captured guidelines for over fifty such topics that will serve to enrich readers with positive outlooks and with concepts and skills that they would otherwise be denied.

Keeping the theme of being better through the self-improvement method in mind, his most recent work includes: "A Symposium on Being an Exceptional Player in the Modern Society (Presented in Seven Short Speeches)," and a much shorter version of these 20 minute speeches, entitled "Seven Concepts for Setting Oneself Apart From Others." It is notable that he has offered the shorter version of speeches to local teen groups at no cost.

Although much could be said about the training articles he has published, his war-fighting innovations, his teaching methods, his painting and golfing hobbies, and his citizenship work, it suffices to state that in every case he added a personal touch to the dimension mentioned while usually setting himself apart from others.

Holland E. Bynam

While it is certain that the aim of *The Exceptional Teenagers' Development League Book* is to open new vistas of thought concerning the building blocks for interpersonal and self-improvement success, it is also certain that the teenagers introduced to these building blocks will have been given the edge they need to become dynamic players in the social, educational, economic, and workplace arenas of the future. Although Colonel Bynam is not alone in thinking that the nation's treasure is embodied in our youthful strivers, and that our most important work is to empower these with special knowledge and skills, he is one of the few who has shown a willingness to fight against the odds in making efforts to build up the teenagers we will depend on in later years with the essential things they need to know for developing wholesomely. If nothing else, this defines him as a visionary patriot with a steady eye aimed on giving younger people an edge for dealing successfully with 21st Century issues and concerns.

Printed in the United States
By Bookmasters